R&D CONSORTIA:

A BENCHMARK STUDY

FRANCIS W. WOLEK
PROFESSOR EMERITUS
VILLANOVA UNIVERSITY

PALANTINE BOOKS
AUDUBON, PENNSYLVANIA
2014

Consortia R&D: A Benchmark Study

A catalog record is pending at the U.S. Library of Congress

ISBN 13: 978-1514236031

Library of Congress Control No.: 2014912545

Cover Graphic: Licensed from iStock Image No. 47811166

For copies of this book, please email: www.francis.wolek@villanova.edu

Table of Contents

List of Tables and Figures

List of Tables and Figures (Cont.)

PREFACE

The title of this book calls it a benchmark; meaning that the data collected and the discussion relates to a specific period of history. That period, the mid-1970s, was one of exceptional activity on national R&D policy. President Carter was elected in 1976 and built on that interest with a host of programs to stimulate science and technology. The initiative of most relevance was a Domestic Policy Review on Industrial Innovation (DPR). The DPR was led by a dynamic advocate for an active role of government in innovation – Dr. Jordan Baruch, Assistant Secretary for Science and Technology at the U.S. Department of Commerce. I was fortunate to be Jordan's Principal Deputy Assistant Secretary and a deputy director for the DPR.

Cooperation between industrial firms on technical innovation was of particular interest to both government and industrial officials at the time of the DPR. Fortunately, I had received a National Science Foundation grant for research on R&D industrial consortia. The report on that grant was a major input into the conceptualization and development of a major new initiative of the Commerce Department: The Cooperative Generic Technology Program (COGENT).

This book is essentially a professional rewrite of my National Science Foundation report. The data and the policy thinking behind the report are the same as the NSF report. This book has neither updated the data nor reconsidered the report's conclusions in light of more recent research and discussion. As such, the book is true to the 1970s in content and tone. That approach is warranted since the intervening time has not been positive for U.S. consortia. Many organizations referenced here no longer exist including several, like the Textile Research Institute and the Institute of Paper Chemistry that were high status leaders.

Portents of the decline existed during this study, for example, the decline of non-energy consortia and Board Directives to abandon basic research. Furthermore, the decline of the general economy was just too much for consortia to weather. It is my firm belief that R&D consortia will indeed rise again when growth returns. However, they will have to correct the weaknesses of their past and build upon their strengths. It is my fond hope that this study will help future leaders, policymakers and scholars improve on the ever promising idea of stimulating productive cooperation on industrial science and technology.

Francis Wolek

June, 2014

Chapter 1

INTRODUCTION

"In one form or another speculative or reflective interest in cooperation is as old as human thought From Confucius, Lao-tze, and Gautama in the Far East as from the prophets of the Old Testament, the centrality of the ethic and psychology of cooperation may be easily inferred. For both Plato and Aristotle, cooperation was the keystone of the good state" (Nisbet, 1968, p. 386)

Cooperation is widely viewed as a good idea. Individual organizations may pursue projects they would not dare do alone. Risky and long-range work might be possible with cooperation. Sharing also has the allure of efficiency in avoiding waste and duplication. In short, pooled effort has appealing potential. Such is the promise, but what is the reality? The substance of that reality is the subject of this book.

Aims of the Study

The immediate purpose of this study was gathering descriptive data on organized cooperation on technological R&D in the United States. The focus of the study was historical in that the data are from the 1970s; a period when policymakers were actively interested in cooperative innovation. The data describe:

a. Functions served by consortia in the innovation process;

b. Differences between cooperative and competitive R&D;

c. Benefits members obtain from consortia;

d. Extent of cooperative R&D by both field and by industry;

e. Organizational structures and procedures used to define, pursue, and use cooperative work; and

f. Managerial lessons about consortia from their formation to their demise.

Scope of the Book

While the study's immediate purpose is descriptive, it also seeks to assist those who manage and set policy on cooperative R&D in industry, academia, and government. One targeted audience was those in government who formulate policy on technological innovation.

As noted in the beginning quote, cooperation is a basic social process. Therefore, the considerable research on this process is not surprising. As this study progressed, it became clear that, questions were being asked that describes the nature, extent, and practices of R&D consortia. However, additional questions were needed to analyze the management of collaborative innovation. Filling this need partly mean dealing with a maxim of social research that 'you can't get fish to describe water'. Managers, the 'fish' in this study, could not describe or analyze their managerial behavior and approaches to cooperation. These basics were developed over so many years and had become such everyday matters that they were taken for granted.

As the relevance of theoretical literature grew, it became evident that managerial processes cannot be taken for granted. The need for a set of principles for the management of cooperation became clear such as for member definition, committee structure, liaison procedure, and rules for agreement and negotiation. In other words, formulating such a setoff management principles needed to be part of this study.

Definition of Consortium

How did this study define 'R&D consortium'? Unfortunately, a satisfactory definition was not identified. Dictionary definitions range from the impossibly broad ('any association') to the impossibly narrow ('international banking cartel'). The most intriguing definition is: 'an intimate association of organisms formed for the purpose of mutual, physical satisfaction'. In lieu of an existing definition, the study used the following:

> *R&D Consortium: A formal association of three or more companies that cooperate in funding and planning technical research and development.*

It was difficult to both locate and make a systematic sample of firm–to–firm partnerships versus one of formal associations that fund and plan multi-project programs. Multiple members supporting multiple projects at a formal consortium differs from a single project partnership such as National Cash Register and Control Data's cooperation on point-of-sale terminals. Another example was the oil industry's Catalytic Research Associates described by Enos (1962) as a series of "entirely separate groups ... deployed on the [existing] problems of better synthetic catalysts, operating conditions for catalytic reaction, and ... patent conflicts."

The Questionnaire Survey

The questionnaire on cooperative R&D was a main source of data (see the Appendix). The questionnaire was mailed to 610 organizations and elicited 331 replies (a 54% return) from 123 organizations conducting R&D. Table 1 summarizes the sample, and Table 2 the variables studied.

Sample Design: The list of organizations receiving questionnaires was compiled from the Encyclopedia of Associations. This standard reference has data on thousands of American associations of national stature. The mailing list was compiled from sections on:

a. Trade, Business, and Commercial Organizations

b. Agricultural Organizations and Commodity Exchanges

c. Scientific, Engineering, and Technical Organizations, and

d. Health and Medical Organizations.

Questionnaires were only sent to organizations whose descriptions implied involvement in scientific and technical R&D with such as references as:

a. R&D programs (examples: funds R&D, runs an R&D program, operates a laboratory),

b. Formal R&D Committees, and

c. Committees possibly focused on Science and Technology (a "Technology Committee").

One item on the questionnaire asked for the names of three consortia in the respondent's field. This question added fourteen organizations to the sample.[1]

---

[1] Ninety-six questionnaires were sent to a random sample of organizations whose descriptions implied no involvement in R&D. Only one return showed R&D activity.

4

Table 1

Questionnaire Sample*

Org. Type	Possible	Surveyed	Replies	%	# w/ R&D	%
Trade	2,800	a) 179	95	53	55	58
		b) 118	70	59	31	44
		c) 97	37	38	10	27
		d) 7	7	100	7	100
Agricultural	600	a) 22	14	64	2	14
		b) 43	19	44	6	32
		c) 3	3	100	0	0
		d) 2	2	100	2	100
Prof. Soc.	800	30	12	40	6	50
Health	1,000	25	6	24	3	50
Random	N/A-	96	68	71	1	1

*a) Cited w/R&D Program, b) Cited w/R&D Committee, c) Cited w/Technical Committee, and d) Cited by Interviewees.

Table 2

Variables Included in the Questionnaire Survey

1. Location of R&D by

    a. Industry or professional specialty (Question 1)[2]
    b. Type of sponsoring organization (Question 3)
    c. Geographic proximity to industrial and academic activity (1, 19)

2. Extent of R&D by

    a. Dollar budget (8)
    b. Growth of dollar budget over the past five years (8)
    c. Importance vs. other activities of the consortium (2,7)
    d. Age of program (6)

3. Nature of R&D by

    a. Involvement in functions in the innovation process (11)
    b. Extent of commitment to basic research (10)
    c. Government and proprietary contracts (12, 17)

4. Organization of R&D by

    a. Funding mechanism used (20)
    b. Location where the R&D is performed (18)
    c. Importance of contracts with and to U.S. government (12-14)
    d. Use of proprietary contracts as a source of support (15-17)
    e. Relationship to of sponsorship (e.g. , university vs. Trade)
    f. Extent of members contribution to R&D (21)
    g. Policies used in dealing with foreign members (22-24)
    h. Source of ideas for R&D projects (25)

----

[2] Numbers refer to questions in the questionnaire.

The sections of the Encyclopedia on Industrial, Trade, and Commercial Organizations, and on Agricultural and Commodity associations were straight forward. Sections on Scientific, Engineering, and Technical professional societies and on Health and Medical organizations were more difficult to interpret. In the former, the description "supports scientific and/or technical research" could refer to non-R&D activities such as organizing scientific meetings and publishing professional journals. Organizations listed in the Health section included many non-member organizations such as government supported institutes and fund-raising foundations. Because of these difficulties, this report is limited to industrial organizations that explicitly fund or conduct an R&D program or operate a laboratory.

Data Obtained: The variables in the questionnaire survey were chosen to describe the location, extent, nature, and organization of R&D at consortia. In formulating the questions, significant assistance was obtained from two previous studies of cooperative R&D [Battelle Institute (1956) and P.S. Johnson (1973)].

Data Validation: Most questions on budget dealt with well-known dollar figures and did not need validation. However, two questions (#11 on the functions of R&D and #25 on the sources of ideas for projects) were based on subjective estimates. The reliability of these data was validated in 25 telephone interviews that asked for the same data and probed any differences. Specific examples of projects that fit the categories in question 11 were also obtained and studied. Data on question 25 was reasonably reliable and valid, but some sources were confused about the definition of fundamental and basic research.

The Interview Survey

Additional data in this study was obtained through interviews (see Table 3). In total, 144 interviews were conducted including 91 interviews at 26 consortia, 20 at industrial firms, four at academic institutions, and three at government agencies. In addition, approximately 50 telephone interviews were conducted at 35 consortia, 12 industrial firms, and three government agencies.

Sample Design: The most intensive interviews were with people in textiles and energy (electric/gas) technology. These interviews were with executives at all major consortia, member companies, nonmember companies, and academic institutions. Further detail about these fields is presented in Table 4 and 5. In addition to textile and electric/gas technologies, interviews were also conducted in the fields of primary metals and agricultural technology.

Table 3
Variables in the Interview Study

1. Role of Consortia in the Innovation Process by

    a. Opinion of all sources
    b. Reference to specific examples of past contributions
    c. Reference to nature of current projects

2. Competitive Nature of R&D Projects by

    a. Characteristics of projects at consortia and member firms (e.g., size, risk, breadth, percentage fundamental research, etc.)
    b. Agreement on differences between consortia and members

3. Relative importance of consortia contributions to innovation by

    a. Opinions of executives of member firms
    b. Subjective evaluation of benefits to member firms

4. Benefits Received by Members of Consortia by

    a. Value received vs. cost of membership for benefits (e.g., original. knowledge, news, opportunities for interaction, etc.)
    b. Correlation of firm innovativeness with involvement in consortia
    c. Type of firm receiving significant benefits plus reasons for this
    d. Correlation of innovativeness and consortia involvement

5. Barriers to Innovative Work at Consortia by

    a. Descriptions of foregone or missed opportunities
    b. Type of procedure for R&D project selection

6. Use of R&D Conducted at Consortia by

    a. Committee purposes, structure and procedures
    b. Type of specific project
    c. Nature of incident involving liaison persons
    d. Kind and the process of dissemination of information

7. Present and Potential Impact of Government on Consortia by

    a. Extent of contribution from government such as change in antitrust legislation)
    b. Case histories of projects of government contracts
    c. Case histories of projects involving government regulation

Table 4
Characteristics of Textile Technology

<u>**Characteristics**</u>	<u>**Analysis Objectives**</u>
1. A large number of companies and a history of R&D consortia operations.	Opportunity to study the success and innovativeness of: consortia members vs. nonmembers and more vs. less involved members.
2. An industrial structure with medium and large companies.	Determine if large vs. small organizations benefit most from consortia R&D and trace member-consortia interaction on benefits. The presence of large firms with established R&D programs permits evaluation of: a. Constraints at large firms on projects paralleled by consortia and b. Overlap in consortia and company R&D programs
3. A mix of different types of consortia: a) university-based, b) association-based, and c) consortia with laboratories, and d) ones that rely on contracted work.	Opportunity for comparative analysis of: a. Activities and role in the innovation process. b. Extent and nature of member benefits.

9

Table 5
Characteristics of Electric and Gas Technology

Characteristics	**Analysis Objectives**
1. A noncompetitive industry where the majority of R&D is carried out by consortia.	Definition and measurement of benefits from cooperative R&D that are not confused by benefits from competitive R&D.
	Comparison of benefits received from more vs. less active members and the processes of member-consortia interaction.
	•
2. An industrial structure with a sample of large and small companies.	Comparison of membership benefits to different types of members such as utility co-ops that might benefit from a similar structure.
3. A mix of consortia types: 1) university based, 2) association based, and 3) independent R&D institutes.	Comparison of activities, benefits, and inter-organizational processes.
4. Electric and Gas technology has complex ties between equipment producers and utility companies	Evaluation of R&D portfolios and processes of R&D to determine if consortia work differently with different organizations and institutions.
5. The federal government gives significant to R&D (e.g., atomic power research) and actively shares in planning for the use of new technologies	Description and qualitative evaluation of the process of government involvement in R&D consortia.
6. A new organization (EPRI) was formed to organize and fund consortia R&D.	Description and analysis of initiating and organizing a new consortium.

10

Data Obtained: Interviews in the selected industries were obtained at consortia, industrial firms, and universities and include: opinions (What is the role of this consortium in innovation in its field?), simple scales of strength of opinion (To what extent would this consortium's contribution be enhanced by changes in antitrust legislation?), and measures of R&D projects (dollar budget).

Context for Research

Two concerns of previous work were relevant to this study: (1) conclusions about government policy and (2) empirical findings on the extent and nature of consortia R&D.

U.S. Government Policy and Consortia: Two factors inspired governmental interest in consortia: First, Consortia were increasingly seen as possible sites for projects that are too large or risky for individual firms. In addition, policymakers recognized that prior work had not differentiated between member-based organizations and focused partnerships on specific projects.

An Economic Report of the President notes:

> "The difficulty of a firm understanding its own R&D efforts may be especially great when the firm is small in relation to the scale required for efficient R&D efforts ... firms may be able to share risks or pool their support of R&D through formal or informal consortia under today's legal and institutional arrangements (1971, p. 127)."

Given the high risk and large investments involved in significant projects, the Commerce Technical Advisory Board felt that a number of industry-government and multi-company cooperative research and development programs should be considered. A related study on industry's perceptions of cooperative research and development concluded "there is a dearth of pertinent cases to guide interested companies." (Industrial Research Institute, 1975, p. 3)

Much of the interest in member-based associations was based on a belief that associations might enhance the application and diffusion of new technology. Examples are the following two quotes:

> "While Great Britain's public support for industrial research associations has been criticized, the United States might explore the underlying idea of connecting universities to association activities. Most industrialized countries other than the United States have used this mechanism to achieve the diffusion of technology. (Hollomon (p.18)"

> "The study also showed that, although many promising R&D programs are being conducted by universities ... no mechanism currently exists for directly translating research results into innovations of practical value to crushed stone operators. It is recommended, therefore, that the National Crushed Stone Association ... expand its role to include technology transfer from laboratories (particularly, university laboratories) to the quarry operators." (Ozol, et al, 1974)

11

Despite speculative interest, sources were unenthusiastic about the potential of consortia and were dissatisfied with the performance of consortia in Western Europe. One example is an influential book on government policy by Nelson, Peck, and Kalachek (1967, p. 191):

> "The authors would be mildly sympathetic to partial government aid for industry cooperative research associations in whatever industry they are formed. Such a program might involve giving governmental support to the formulation of industry organized research cooperatives either through tax credits or government grants that match the contributions from the firms in the industry ... The English experience indicates that the cooperatives have been useful in performing applied research on industry-wide problems like the maintenance of equipment, or common manufacturing problems. They have been useful in testing and evaluating materials and in distributing technical information. But as an effective source of far-reaching developments they have proved a disappointment."

Empirical Studies of R&D Consortia in Europe: Most European studies are of research associations (RAs) in England (Johnson, Jones, and Woodward). As Woodward noted (1965, p. 47), the organization of RAs differs widely and each country has its own approach to membership, funding, and government representation. Nevertheless, a few findings were found generally valid:

a. Consortia receive greater support in non-technology intensive industries and where members lack, private R&D programs.

b. Members receive a fair return on their contributions to consortia and the work of consortia is believed valuable to technical progress.

c. Consortia make neither major nor notable contributions.

d. The most valued benefits are technical services to members such as information services, education, consultation, and testing that promote improvements of existing technology.

e. There are organizational barriers to accomplishing major tasks cooperatively.

f. Larger consortia that operate their own laboratories play significant roles in their industries and attract and retain competent staffs.

Woodward's (p. 37) study concludes that: "There is no doubt whatsoever ... that the RAs have performed and are performing a very considerable service to industry." This study (p. 36) summarizes the purposes of RAs:

a. Make their industry research-conscious.

b. Investigate problems of interest to a major sector of an industry that cannot be undertaken by a single member.

c. Transmit new research and technical 'know-how' to the industry.

d. Stimulate small and medium firms without research facilities.

e. Save money in using scientific manpower."

Jones (1972) agrees with Woodward on the purposes of the RAs, however, he feels strongly that a change of purposes and outlook is needed. Jones notes that there has been a growth in "repayment work"[3] and states (p. 67) that;

> "It is the primary conclusion of this study that those RAs which have over the last ten years attempted to break away from the traditional formula, to become more oriented towards specific industrial demand and less towards a cooperative style of activity, have interpreted the contemporary climate correctly and taken a major step towards ensuring for themselves an effective future existence."

Jones (p. 88) concludes that:

> "Associations should increasingly order their technical activities on the basis of direct commissioning by members and project-linked payments. This will involve, in particular, group projects and repayment work. The importance of a general programme determined by the intermediary of an elected Council or research committee, and not by direct member-demands, should diminish. ... Membership should cease to involve programme-control as one of its central benefits. Membership should convey primarily the right of preferential, though not necessarily exclusive, access to RA services."

Johnson's study (1973) presents the most detailed findings on activities of RAs and concludes (p. 206) with a strong note of "uncertainty about the future (of RAs), and in some cases even their existence." This uncertainty is traced to three sources:

a. Unease that RAs are "neither wholly private nor wholly public,"

b. Dissatisfaction that "RAs have not been responsible for many important technological breakthroughs", and

c. Confusion that "RAs serve industries which contain widely different technological interests".

Johnson agrees with Jones on "greater specificity in industrial subscriptions" and encouraging multi-client contracts. However, Johnson (pp. 206-7) notes:

> "It may be argued that it is not the RAs' function to undertake work of direct commercial importance to members; rather that their objective should be to concentrate on 'complimentary' areas of work in which members are happy to collaborate ... Basic research might also provide another area where firms would be willing to cooperate, although here the RAs compete with the resources of the universities and of government establishments for which industry does not have to pay. In the writer's view the recent change of emphasis in government policy away from regarding basic research as a proper activity of the RAs is a correct one."

In summary all sources note that RAs have not been notably important to technological progress. However, Woodward feels that RAs have nevertheless played

---

[3] Jones found that repayment work was 14.1% of total RA income in 1963 and 25.6% in 1970 (p. 30).

an important role. Jones agrees but feels this role could be enhanced if RAs took on more applied work. Johnson feels that the role of RAs has been misconceived and that they will prove useful when their proper function is better understood.

Empirical Studies of R&D Consortia in the U.S.: The two prior studies of R&D consortia in the United States are: a Battelle study and another by the U.S. Senate. Both studies present findings similar to work on European RAs.

The survey of the Battelle Institute (1956) specifically addressed the importance of government policy on consortia. After reviewing this question in interviews at consortia, the survey concluded that:

> "The direct conclusion of this rather negative response is that Federal legislation, regulations, and agencies apparently have little or no effect on cooperative research. Antitrust actions at one time a popular 'bug-a-boo' of trade associations seem a thing of the past … If any feeling at all is projected it is that a minimum governmental regulation and supervision are desired." (p. 28)

The Senate report had a focus on the patent system but confirmed Battelle's conclusion. A conference sponsored by the Department of Commerce Technical Advisory Board (Industrial Research Institute, 1975) recommended clarifications in antitrust policy on cooperative R&D. These clarifications would assure that cooperative R&D did not limit competition in an industry (example: the results of cooperative R&D should be available to the public at large). These recommendations will be discussed in a later chapter dealing with U.S. government policy.

Summary

Cooperation has attracted attention as a way to pursue long-range, risky work difficult for single firms. Yet cooperation has not yielded major advances in either other countries or in the U.S.

Chapter 2

WHO DOES COOPERATIVE R&D AND WHY

"(This) is a record of our search ..., for some of the reasons that individuals do not cooperate more. Our negative phrasing of the problem – why don't people cooperate more – is not accidental. It is our conviction that although examples of interpersonal cooperation may be easily found, individualism in goal achievement is much more common in this, and in probably every other society" (Marwell and Schmitt, 1975, p.2)

Cooperation is generally desired. From early childhood we are urged to cooperate and to exhibit a 'team spirit'. Yet, study after study finds that effective cooperation is elusive, temporary, and limited. This chapter shows that cooperation does occur and that we can study the conditions where it flourishes and makes valuable contributions.

Who Does Cooperative R&D?

Tables 6 and 7 show the extent of cooperative R&D in the U.S. Table 8 on cooperative R&D in both the U.S. and in England supports two observations. First, energy related industries are highly important with seventy percent of R&D funds.[4] Second, 'R&D intensive' industries such as electronics and pharmaceuticals lack cooperative programs.

The importance of cooperative R&D in nontechnical industries is confirmed in Figure 1 (top) showing an inverse relationship[5] on the importance of cooperative R&D versus the importance of R&D for industries other than in Energy. A corresponding relationship exists for cooperative R&D in England (see the bottom panel in Figure 1).

---

[4] Emphasis on energy R&D will become stronger. The Electric Power Research Institute has an R&D program that equals spending on cooperative R&D by all other consortia. The gas industry is expanding an R&D in a counterpart of EPRI called the Gas Research Institute (GRI).

[5] The inverse relationship of cooperative R&D to the importance of R&D is evident in the regression lines of Figure 1. The Spearman coefficients were: England = 0.79 (t=4.84, p =<.001); U.S. = 0.73 (t=3.88, p =<.001). The full data show that English industries devoted roughly 8% more of their total R&D to cooperative R&D than the U.S.

Table 6

Extent of Cooperative R&D by U.S. Industry in 1974*

SIC	Industry	Coop R&D ($000)	% R&D	Ind. R&D** ($M)	% Sales
20	**Food**	3.870	1.32	293	0.39
21	**Tobacco**	NR	NR	36	0.38
22	**Textiles**	0.919	1.51	61	0.45
23	**Apparel**	0.000	0	0.21	
24	**Lumber & Wood**	0.806	2.37	34	0.52
25	**Furniture**	NR	NR	31	0.88
26	**Paper**	3.880	1.78	218	0.67
27	**Printing**	2.032	5.98	34	0.61
28	**Chemicals**	1.112	0.05	2,148	3.44
29	**Petroleum**	3.789	0.66	578	0.64
30	**Rubber**	NR	NR	261	1.58
31	**Leather**	0.113	1.26	9	0.52
32	**Stone, Clay, & Glass**	2.627	1.40	187	1.44
33	**Primary Metals**	5.236	1.70	308	0.56
34	**Fabricated Metals**	0.235	0.08	274	1.13
35	**Machinery**	0.040	0	2,134	3.22
36	**Electrical Equipment**	0.010	0	2,892	3.51
37	**Transportation Equip.**	2.935	0.140	2,112	2.80
38	**Instruments**	0.080	0	824	4.44
39	**Miscellaneous Mfg.**	0.085	NA	NA	NA
49	**Electric & Gas**	51.327	54.03	95	0.68
	Avg. & Total	79.096	0.63	12,536	1.89

* Table 7 presents data on cooperative R&D supported by U.S. industry only excluding income from foreign and U.S. government sources. Table 8 presents data on total R&D of consortia.

** Total R&D in the industry; Source: NSF Highlights, 1976 (NSF 76-300)

Table 7

Extent of R&D at Consortia

Industry	Consortia R&D ($000)	Percent
Electric and gas	61,999	51.9
Mining (Coal)	18,117	15.2
Primary Metals	6,895	5.8
Railroads	5,660	4.7
Paper	3,880	3.3
Food	3,697	3.1
Petroleum	3,719	3.1
Stone, Clay, and Glass	3,222	2.7
Transportation Equipment	2,935	2.5
Environmental	2,289	2.0
Printing	1,962	1.6
Chemicals	977	0.8
Textiles	945	0.8
Lumber & Wood	847	0.7
Construction	599	0.5
Inter-industry Councils	512	0.4
Services	440	0.4
Fabricated Metals	111	0.2
Leather	113	0.1
Miscellaneous Manufacturing	85	0.1
Instruments	80	0.1
Machinery	40	
Electrical Equipment	10	
Totals	$119,323	100 %

Table 8

Comparison of U.S. and English Cooperative R&D

U.S.		England	
Industry	**% Coop.**	**Industry**	**% Coop.**
Electric & Gas	54.0	Ships	32.4
Printing	6.0	Apparel & Leather	26.3
Lumber & Wood	2.4	Construction	13.7
Paper	1.8	Non-Ferrous Metals	11.3
Primary Metals	1.5	Textiles & Fibers	10.9
Textiles	1.5	Wood & Paper	9.9
Stone, Clay & Glass	1.4	Rubber	8.0
Food	1.3	Iron & Steel	7.3
Leather	1.3	Stone & Clay	7.1
Petroleum	0.7	Instruments	5.6
Transportation Equip.	0.1	Metal Products	5.0
		Food & Tobacco	4.3
		Chemicals	1.8
		Plastics	1.2
		Motor Vehicles	1.1

Figure 1
Relationship of Cooperative R&D to Total R&D

United States

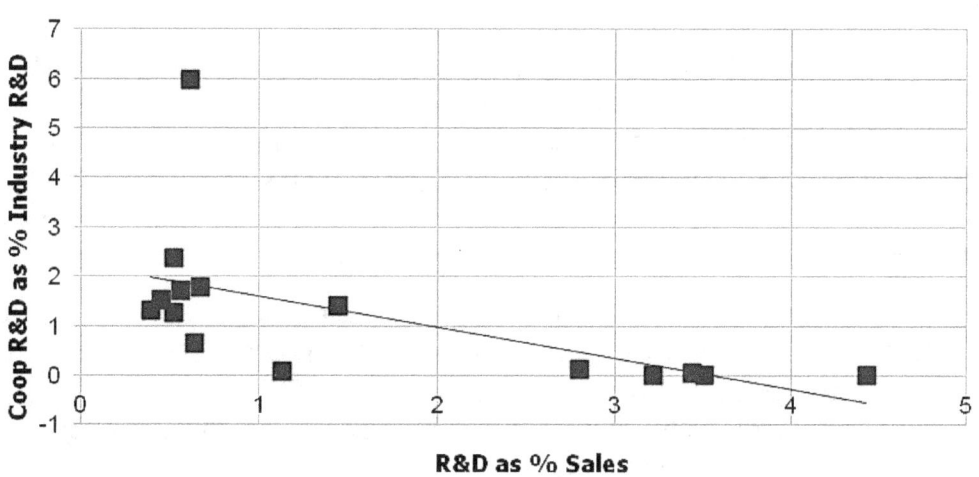

England

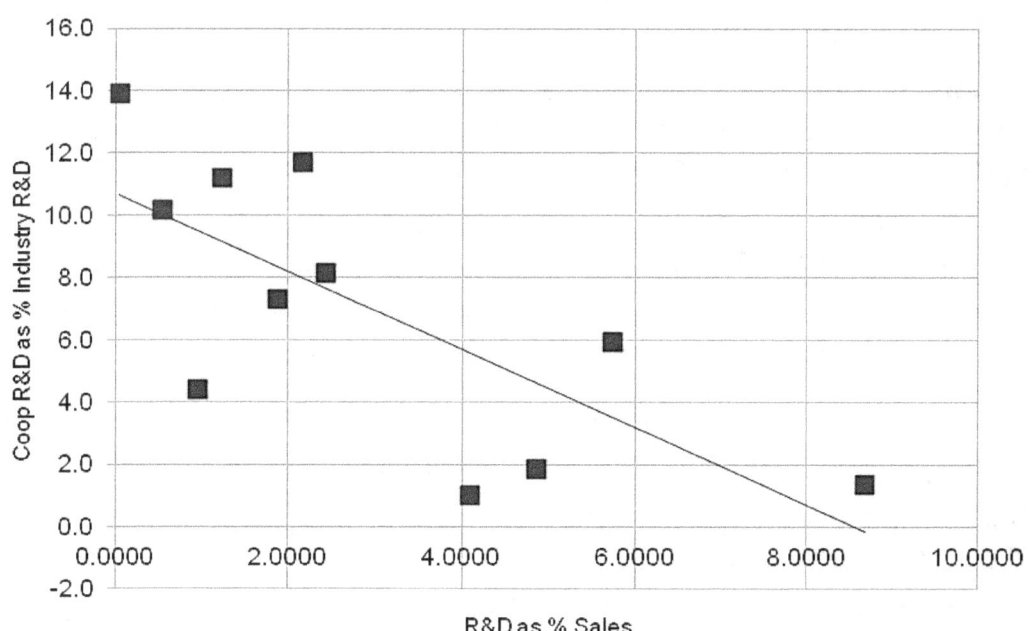

Why Do Industries Support Cooperative R&D?

Interviews and the literature agree that two conditions exist for supporting cooperative R&D: 1) significant **Uniformity** over time and among firms in technology, and 2) **Threat** to the industry.

An example of uniformity's influence is the cement industry. Despite intense competition on cost and delivery performance, the cement industry has the 12th largest cooperative program in this survey. An example of the importance of threat is the synthetic fiber industry. Uniformity is not a factor there since R&D is important in competition between fiber companies. But threat of public uproar about fabric flammability prompted a significant cooperative program.

The apparel industry is an example on the absence of cooperative R&D. The industry received significant government support for a cooperative R&D program. However, the industry had great difficulty defining common needs for R&D. Technical performance is not competitively important but fashion is and fashion changes limited the emergence of uniform production and marketing technologies.

Cooperative R&D may not emerge in highly uniform fields if significant threat is absent. For example, water utilities have highly uniform services and technology. However, unlike electric power, which faced severe threats (e.g., environmental challenges and alternative energy sources), water companies have not faced industry threats and do not cooperate on R&D.

The Importance of Uniformity in Technology: Difficulties are great when those in diverse industrial and geographic contexts seek to cooperate. Uniformity in products and production processes reduces these organizational costs:

  a. Communication is facilitated by common language and history – (Litwak and Hylton, 1962; Inzerilli, 1975),

  b. "Unfair" advantage and Domain Dominance concerns are dampened — (Marwell and Schmidt, 1975; Deutsch, 1973, Van de Ven, 1975),

  c. R&D goals become similar – (Deutsch, 1949, Schermerhorn, 1975),

  d. Supplier marketing programs may promote common identity,

  e. Private returns become possible from services such as journals, conventions, and statistical services; and

  f. Prior association reduces the costs of new benefits such as R&D (Olson, 1965).[6]

---

[6] Reviews on inter-organizational cooperation may also be found in Schermerhorn, 1975; Van de Ven, 1975b; Tuite, Grisholm, and Radnor, 1972.

The Importance of Common Threat: Theory on the importance of a common threat argues that this factor also reduces the costs of cooperation:

a. In normal circumstances, members may have different goals. External threat motivates a common and an urgent focus on communication.

b. Collective action focuses tension on a common challenge. (Blau and Scott, 1962; and Tach,1965)

c. Threat promotes common identity and cohesiveness. (Schein, 1973, Tach, 1965; and Wilson, 1973)

d. Communication increases with stress and uncertainty. (Bodensteiner, 1970)

e. Simple approaches to interaction are accepted. (Tach, 1965, Wilson, 1973)

The "Economic Theory of Collective Goods" (Olson, 1965) argues that, if a subset of members cooperate to share a collective good, others will contribute as little as possible since they already have access. In other words, other members prefer a "free ride" to cooperative funding. Threat decreases this preference since it places the survival of all in question (Olson and Zeckhauser, 1966).

Why should corporate executives even think of projects beyond their individual goals? Social scientists agree that common threat motivates all to minimize the perceived disparity between foreseen and desired circumstances. Threat from a common source not only creates disparity but, since it lies outside ordinary circumstances, calls for extraordinary action (Wilson, 1973 and Turk, 1973).

Feelings of uncertainty also motivate people to join groups. Festinger, 1967; Schacter, 1969; and Schatz, 1972, argue that people are more likely to recognize feelings by comparison with others and that such comparison encourages affinitive action. Effective response to threat may also require collective strength. Even the largest, single member may be too small to respond to threats to survival such as Dutch Elm disease. (Schemerhorn, 1975; Mott, 1968)

The importance of external threat was present in the founding of British RAs. P.S. Johnson (1973, p. 19-20), noted that the system was born after the manpower drains of World War I produced widespread concern about England's competitive status in world markets. This concern about whether private R&D was adequate led government to underwrite a system for cooperative R&D.

A second example is from one of the oldest R&D consortia in the U.S., the Hawaiian Sugar Research Association. This organization was formed in 1895 to respond to a crop disease threatening industry destruction. R&D sponsored by the Association yielded the sought for cure of the disease (Battelle Institute, 1956). A final example is the largest American R&D consortium: the Electric Power Research Institute. Several students of this organization (e.g., Gordon, 1973) propose that it was motivated by Congressional threats to nationalize R&D on atomic power.

Is Cooperative R&D Growing?

Four consortia in energy-based industries have had exceptional growth (the Electric Power Research Institute, the American Gas Association, the Institute of Gas Technology, and Bituminous Coal Research, Inc.). In fact, these organizations constitute over 60% of total R&D consortia in the 1970s. Therefore, a true picture of cooperative R&D must separate out these and one related consortium (Target, Inc.) from the remainder of industrially R&D consortia.

Aggregate Growth of Cooperative R&D: Table 9 shows that total expenditures for cooperative R&D in the U.S. grew by 84% over five years. This growth compares favorably with a growth of 21% in total R&D in the U.S. and 19% in industrially supported R&D[7]. However, after adjusting for inflation, total U.S. R&D expenditures decreased by 4% and industrial expenditures decreased by 6%. By comparison, inflation-adjusted cooperative R&D increased by 59%.

Table 9

Aggregate Growth in Cooperative R&D ($000) *

Year	R&D Total	% Annually	Cum %
1970	$54,148	-	-
1971	58,244	7.6	7.6
1972	67,362	15.7	24.4
1973	70,709	5.0	30.6
1974	99,838	41.2	84.4

*Data presented here differ from Table 8 because the latter include data from annual reports.

The strong growth (190%) in energy-based consortia distorts the total industrial picture. Cooperative R&D in other fields was virtually stagnant; only 7.5% in five years (see Table 10). After correction for inflation, non-energy cooperative R&D decreased significantly by 17.5%.

---

7 Source: National Science Foundation, National Patterns of R&D Resources, 1974.

Table 10

Growth in Energy vs. General Industry R&D

($000)

A. Energy Consortia (not Petroleum)

Year	Total R&D $	%/yr. Inc.	% over 1970
1970	$22,787	-	-
1971	28,461	24.9	24.9
1972	38,595	28.6	60.6
1973	39,358	7.6	72.7
1974	66,117	68.0	190.2

B. General Industry

Year	Total R&D $	%/yr. Inc.	% over 1970
1970	$31,361	-	-
1971	29,783	-5.0	-5.0
1972	30,757	3.3	-1.9
1973	31,351	1.9	0.0
1974	33,721	7.6	7.5

Association of Growth with Consortia Characteristics: Table 11 shows an association between growth and: (1) importance of R&D, (2) percent of budget for R&D, and (3) size of program. Growing consortia also conduct R&D in their own laboratories (Table 12). The final association (Table 13) is that ideas for projects at growing programs originate with consortia staffs rather than member companies or outside contractors. Significant associations were not found between growth and program age or basic research commitment.

23

Table 11

Growth in Consortia R&D vs. Importance of R&D*

A. Relative to Other Consortia Functions **

	Growing Programs	Other Programs
R&D is a Primary Function	78	39
R&D is Second or Third	22	41
	100% (N=45)	100% (N=29)

$\chi^2 = 2.25$, p = 0.13

B. Relative to Total R&D Budget ***

	Growing Programs	Other Programs
< 35%	57	77
>= 35%	43	23
	100% (N=42)	100% (N=26)

$\chi^2 = 1.95$, p = 0.16

C. Relative to Size of R&D Budget

	Growing Programs	Other Programs
$45,000/year or larger	76	52
<$45,000/year	24	48
	100% (N=45)	100% (N=29)

$\chi^2 = 3.485$, p = 0.06

* Any increase in R&D comparing 1974 to 1970
** Based on Question 2 of the questionnaire
*** Based on Question 7 of the questionnaire

Table 12
Growth vs. Location of R&D*

Location of R&D	Growing Centers	Non-Growth
Own Laboratory	40	17
Universities	30	34
Profit & Non-Profit Labs	19	28
Other	11	21
	100%	100%
	(N=37)	(N=29)

X^2 =3.15, p = 0.08 (Own Lab vs. All Others). Other tabulations are not significant.

Based on Question 18 of the Questionnaire.

Table 13
Growth vs. Origin of R&D Ideas*

Origin of R&D Ideas	Growth Centers	Non-Growth
Consortium Staff	55	29
Member Representatives	26	42
Others & Mix	19	29
	100%	100%
	(N=42)	(N=28)

χ^2 = 3.64, p = 0.06 **

* Based on Question 25 of the questionnaire. The stated origin was at least 20% higher than others.

** Chi Square was based on a 2x2 table (Staff vs. other origins). The 3x2 χ^2 was 4.69, p = 0.10.

25

Eighteen consortia with budgets over $100,000 grew at more than 25% over the period 1970-1974 which is also faster than the rate of inflation. Sixteen of the 18 rated R&D as their primary function and 10 of 16 consortia emphasized work at their own laboratories.[8] Staff origination of programs was even stronger with 12 of 17 growing consortia relying on staff versus two on representative origination and three on other sources.

Characteristics of Consortia: The average age of consortia was 25 years with a median of 20 years. The average budget was $1 million and the median $70,000. However, many consortia: 1) have budgets less than $10,000, 2) conduct single projects, or 3) only perform intermittent programs. Including small programs in the total sample would distort the picture of cooperative R&D. The survey conducted by the Battelle Institute in 1956 overestimated cooperative R&D by including small programs. The problem was compounded by including diverse groups such as agricultural cooperatives such as Sunkist.

A better view of cooperative R&D only includes industrial consortia with significant budgets. The resulting count of 56 organizations in the Battelle study is much closer to this study's 53 consortia with budgets over $60,000. A list of significant and established programs in both surveys appears in Table 14.

---

[8] Half of the 18 allocated at least 1/3 of their total funds to R&D whereas only 1/5 of non-growing consortia had 1/3 of their funds in R&D.

Table 14
Significant R&D Consortia

Electric Power Research Institute

Bituminous Coal Research

American Gas Association*

Institute of Gas Technology*

Cotton, Inc.

American Assoc. of Railroads

Target

American Institute of Steel & Iron

American Petroleum Institute

Motor Vehicle Manufacturers Association

Institute of Paper Chemistry

Portland Cement Association

Coordinating Research Council

International Lead & Zinc Research Org.

International Copper Research Assoc.

Nat'l Council - Paper, Air & Stream

American Newspaper Publishers Assoc.

National Canners Association

American Plywood Association

Textile Research Institute

National Center for Resource Recovery

Metal Properties Council

Beet Sugar Development Fund

Nutrition Foundation

Graphic Arts Technical Foundation

Malting Barley Improvement Association

National Dairy Council

Institute of Textile Technology

Tile Council of America

Gravure Research Institute

International Fabricare Institute

Manufacturing Chemists Association

Int'l Assoc. Plumbing & Mechanical Off.

Gas Processors Association

Cosmetics, Fragrances & Toiletries Assn.

Brick Institute of America

American Institute of Baking

National Restaurant Association

Western Highway Institute

Soap and Detergent Association·

Paint Research Institute

National Asphalt Pavement Association

National Lime Association

Cast Iron Pipe Research Association

Sulfur Institute

American Cocoa Research Institute

National Crushed Stone Association

Glass Container Research Corporation

National Concrete Masonry Association

American Concrete Pipe Association

Wine Institute

National Claypipe Institute

* Most R&D projects were merged into the Gas Research Institute in 1976.

Association of Size and Age with Consortia Characteristics: Associations with size and age of consortia (presented on Tables 15 through18), for the most part, parallel those with program growth. The larger and older programs are also more important (Table15). Larger, but not older programs, allocate greater shares of budget to R&D (Table 16) and their programs originate with consortia staff (Table 17). The larger, but not older, programs stress work at a consortium laboratory with less reliance on universities (Table 18).

Table 15

Size & Age vs. Importance of R&D

Association with Size

Importance of R&D	Budget >$45,000	Budget <$45,000
R&D is a Primary Function	81	47
R&D is Secondary or Tertiary	19	53
	100%	100%
	(N=53)	(N=30)

$\chi^2 = 9.04$, p = 0.003

Association with Age

Importance of R&D	> 10 Years Old	< 10 Years Old
R&D is a Primary Function	74	53
R&D is Secondary or Tertiary	26	47
	100%	100%
	(N=76)	(N=19)

$\chi^2 = 2.26$, p = 0.13

Table 16

Size vs. % R&D

	Size of R&D Budget *			
% R&D*	**<$45,000**	**$45K − 200K**	**$200K − 1M**	**>$1 M**
Less than 6%	46	21	10	-
Between 6 & 80%	50	71	60	57
Greater than 80%	4	8	30	43
	100% (N=28)	100% (N=24)	100% (N=10)	100% (N=14)

χ^2 = 21.94, p = 0.001

* Data are based on Question 8a of the questionnaire.

Table 17

Size & Age vs. Origin of Ideas

Association with Size *

	Size of Budget	
Origin	**<$45,000**	**>$45,000**
Consortium Staff	11	56
Member Reps	60	22
Other	29	22
	100% (N=28)	100% (N=50)

χ^2 = 17.07, p = <0.001

Association with Age

	Age of Program		
Origin	**< 10 Years**	**10 − 40 Years**	**> 40 Years**
Consortium Staff	12	41	52
Member Reps	53	24	38
Other	35	35	10
	100% (N=17)	100% (N=46)	100% (N=21)

χ^2 = 11.37, p = <0.02

Table 18

Size & Age vs. Location of Work

Association with Size *

| | Size of Program | | |
Location	<$45,000	$45 – 200K	> $200K
Consortium's Lab	12	28	52
Universities	44	32	9
Other	44	40	39
	100%	100%	100%
	(N=25)	(N=25)	(N=23)

$\chi^2 = 11.88$, p = <0.02

Association with Age *

| | Age of Program | | |
Origin	< 10 Years	10 – 40 Years	> 40 Years
Consortium' Lab	7	27	36
Universities	36	37	23
Other	57	36	41
	100%	100%	100%
	(N=14)	(N=45)	(N=22)

$\chi^2 = 5.09$, p = <0.28

Associations are present between size and age and origin of programs and between size and growth. Larger programs tend to be older (Table 19) and growing (Table 20). Detailed examination of the data shows that very large programs (budgets over $1 million) are equally divided in terms of growth and stagnation. No association was found between either size or age and commitment to basic research.

Table 19

Size vs. Age

	Size			
Age	**<$45,000**	**$45K – 200K**	**$200K – 1M**	**>$1M**
<10 years	28	21	10	7
10 – 40 yrs.	55	51	60	50
>40 years	17	28	30	43
	100%	100%	100%	100%
	(N=29)	(N=24)	(N=10)	(N=14)

$\chi^2 = 5.07$, p = <0.63 *

*While the association lacks statistical significance, the consistent rise and decline of percentages suggests association.

Table 20

Size and Growth

	Size of Program			
Growth of R&D	**<$45,000**	**$45K-200K**	**$200K-1M**	**>$1M**
Positive	44	74	88	50
Zero or Negative	56	26	12	50
	100%	100%	100%	100%
	(N=25)	(N=27)	(N=8)	(N=14)

$\chi^2 = 7.97$, p = <0.05

Those Who Don't Do R&D and Why Not

Interviews at thirty-one consortia without R&D indicated that some R&D planning is performed project-by-project (see Table 21). One national, farm-animal association conducted a survey of interest in R&D but it was devoted to issues of animal health. The American Textile Manufacturers Institute (ATMI) did not fund a continuous program but did fund occasional projects as threats arose on such issues such as mill effluent and a cotton dust disease called Byssinosis.

Table 21
Forms of R&D Consideration

Form of Consideration	N	%
Specific projects conducted in the past	12	56
Projects considered but not funded	6	29
Survey of member interest	1	5
Informal consideration by staff	1	5
Unknown	1	5
	21	100%

Barriers to Cooperative R&D: The most significant barrier to cooperative R&D is an inability to define attractive projects requiring cooperation (Table 22). In only two cases was a lack of funds a barrier. In one such case, the organization (a national farm animal association) did conduct initial R&D and knew of possibilities for projects but decided the projects exceeded its means. Instead of cooperative R&D, both associations relied on the R&D of government laboratories.

Table 22
Perceived Barriers to Cooperative R&D

Barrier	N	%
Unable to define relevant projects	7	37
Members prefer doing competitive projects	6	32
Other uses of funds are more worthwhile	3	16
Funds are insufficient for worthwhile projects	2	11
Members prefer suppliers to do projects	1	5
	19	100%

Nature of the R&D Considered: The kinds of projects considered by consortia (Table 23) document the importance of uniformity and, to a lesser extent, threat as motivators of cooperative R&D.[9] All projects were in two categories: a) improvement of common materials or b) responses to anticipated regulations. In three cases, the two categories overlapped since the materials involved (water and meat) had a direct impact on public health and were under active government scrutiny. In four cases of safety-oriented projects, the strength of the threat was insufficient for funding.

It is clear that cooperative industrial R&D is not a great idea waiting for enlightened action. It is also clear that government, is not a barrier to cooperative action. The main barriers are inability to see sufficient value and inability to manage corporate secrets during cooperation.

Table 23

Projects Considered and/or Undertaken

Project Related To	N	%
Government Regulations	4	27
Safety Improvement	4	27
Public Health & Safety	3	20
Materials Commonly Used by Members	3	20
Commonly Used Processes & Equipment	1	6
	15	100%

Summary

Cooperative R&D in the 1970s was a small, but nontrivial, part of R&D in the United States. Consortia spent over $100 million annually on such programs with most being by energy industries such as electric and gas that grew by 190% over five years while expenditures in other fields remained stable. In addition to energy, cooperative R&D was most prominent in non-technology intensive industries especially those experiencing a threat from outside sources such as regulatory pressure, resource scarcity, disease, etc. Consortia that grew were ones in which: 1) cooperative R&D was an already established function, 2) R&D was conducted at the consortium's laboratories, and 3) ideas for projects were generated by the consortium's own staff.

---

[9] These projects concerned: 1) fireproofing of materials, 2) a device to warn equipment operators of dangerous conditions, 3) determining the causes of accidents, and 4) methods of testing for soil conditions on the site of construction projects.

Chapter 3

THE WORK OF CONSORTIA

Although the R.A.s may have been responsible for few major technological breakthroughs, this in itself does not necessarily justify criticism of them, for several reasons. Firstly, much of technological advance is in any case made up of a large number of improvements. Secondly, data on the relationship between major innovations and expenditure in industry and other R&D establishments are required before it can be said that R.A.s are not producing as many innovations as might be expected from the resources they utilize. This information is not available. Thirdly, it may not be the objective of the RA to produce such advances. Is it therefore justifiable to consider them on a criterion that does not conform to their own aims?" (Johnson)

Past studies on R&D consortia conclude with both disappointment and admiration. Investigators admire the dedicated and competent staffs but are disappointed that they produce neither innovative nor significant work. This survey yields similar results and could adopt the same disappointed admiration. However, as Johnson notes, disappointment would be based on inappropriate expectations. Disappointment overlooks admirable contributions to progress that facilitate others' R&D and promotes the use of important technologies.

The Context for R&D

This study divides consortia into two categories: a) Contractors of R&D to outside organizations and b) organizations that sponsor their own laboratories (Table 24). In addition to R&D, both categories engage in a variety of useful activities (Table 25). The importance of communications, for example, is clear as is training member employees. Several Laboratories also have important academic roles and[10] work on government regulations on occupational health and public health and safety issues is also significant.

---

[10] Four of these organizations are located near major universities and offer degree-granting educational programs (Textile Research Institute, Institute of Textile Technology, Institute of Gas Technology, and Institute of Paper Chemistry).

Table 24

Types of R&D Consortia

Type	N	%
R&D Contractor	87	80
Consortia Laboratory	22	20
	109	100%

Consortia R&D and the Innovation Process

Technological innovation is not a simple event; it is a multifaceted process with a variety of leverage points that influence success. R&D consortia are involved in all aspects of this process.

The Functions of R&D and U.S. Consortia: Table 26 describes the functions of consortia projects and emphasizes improving existing technology. Table 27 reinforces the importance of existing technology[11] and that table also shows that consortia have strong commitments to work on regulatory issues (called Social Technology here). Examples include work on occupational and public health such as on mill effluents, air pollution, and factory noise. Put another way, consortia are concerned with issues that may threaten their industry's profitability.

---

11 Several consortia had multiple functions on at least 40% of projects.

Table 25

Importance of Consortia Activities

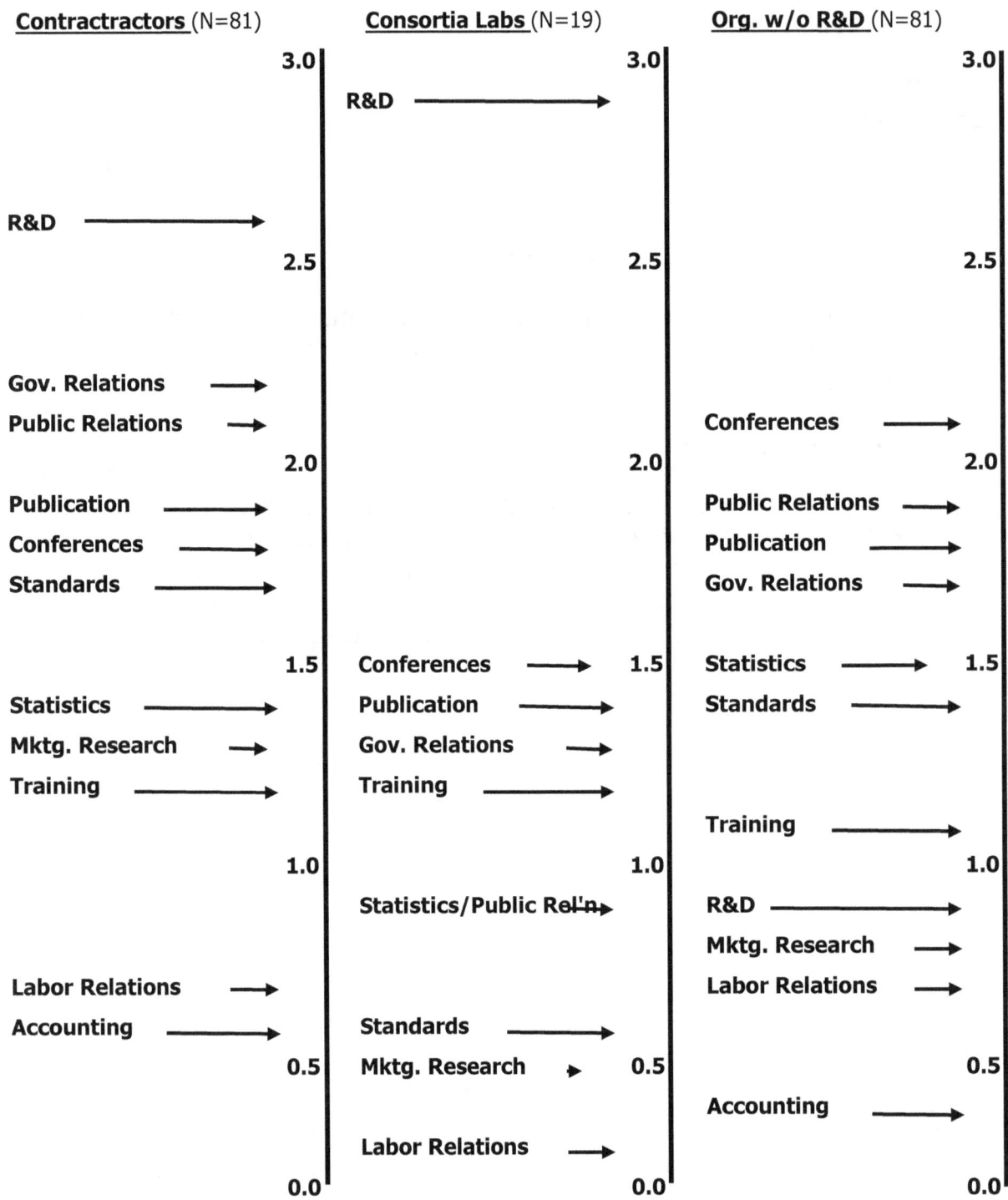

Table 26
Functions of Consortia R&D

Question 11 ID*	Function	% Involvement
A	Exploring Common Material & Processes	28.9
C	Improving Existing Process Technology	26.0
E	Improving Existing Product Technology	25.9
M	Consulting on Technical Operations & Problems	20.1
I	Improving Environmental& Consumer Technology	19.2
G	Improving Occupational & Health Technology	18.4
O	Reporting on Outside Science & Technology	15.1
H	Developing Environmental & Safety Technologies	14.8
L	Developing Material, Process, and Product Tests	14.4
J	Developing Public Health & Safety Standards	13.0
P	Aiding Outsiders to Transfer Technology to the Ind.	12.9
N	Evaluating Outside Technology Developments	11.0
F	Developing Occupational Health & Safety Prototypes	10.8
K	Developing Purchasing or Usage Standards	10.5
Q	Planning to Integrate Different Technologies	10.5
B	Developing Hardware Prototypes for Manufacturing	8.8
D	Developing New Product Prototypes	8.3

* The capital letters are categories listed on Question 11 of the Questionnaire.

Table 27

Types of Programs

Type of Program	N	%	($000) Budget	$ %
Improvement & Social Technology*	18	18.3	33,235	40.4
Improvement of Existing Technology**	11	11.2	20,805	25.3
Scatter of Functions***	16	16.3	6,826	8.3
Social Technology & Basic Studies	5	5.1	6,102	7.4
Social Technology Only	10	10.2	4,110	5.1
Hardware Development & Social Technology	3	3.1	4,020	4.9
Basic Studies	13	13.3	2,144	2.6
Improvement & Hardware Development	4	4.1	1,864	2.3
Consulting & Technology Transfer	5	5.1	1,373	1.7
Hardware Development	4	4.1	1,254	1.5
Improvement & Basic Studies	8	8.2	384	0.5
Hardware Development & Basic Studies	1	1.0	-	-
	98	100%	$82,167	100%

* At least 40% of projects in categories C or E plus with F, or G, or H, or I, or J of Question 11.

** At least 40% of projects in categories C or E alone of Question 11.

*** Significant involvement in more than two categories.

The Functions of R&D at European Consortia: European studies of consortia also stress improvement of existing technology. For example, Johnson writes about RAs:

> "Firstly, in contrast with industry, RAs do little development work. Secondly, many RAs pursue research into standards, measurement and testing methods, and health and safety which, while important, is not of direct commercial relevance to member firms. Finally, the majority of research activities have in the main resulted in cost reductions within the broadly given state of technology."

While Johnson notes that RAs conduct R&D on health and safety issues, his study lacks the emphasis found here. This lesser focus on health and safety may be because RAs were studied before this function became prominent. European members may also lack the fear Americans sense of government threat to industry.

Characteristics of R&D Projects

Data on the projects of consortia are in two forms: 1) opinions about the project characteristics and 2) descriptive data on specific projects.

Opinions of Consortia R&D: Table 28 shows that both consortia staffs and members agree consortia R&D differs from the work of members. The small sample size does not allow definitive conclusions. However, most sources feel that consortia programs are at least equal in size, riskiness, breadth, and planning horizon.[12] The situation for gas and electric consortia is that consortia projects are larger, riskier, broader and more long termed. Consortia in all industries are seen as performing work that is important but lacking in competitive significance.

It is important to note that the 'typical' firm in the studied industries does little or no R&D. For example, a $150 million textile firm widely regarded as innovative had an R&D staff of two full and one half-time professionals. A source in the gas industry noted that only 20 of 300 major companies had an R&D budget. Of those 20, only five supported a formal R&D department. In this context, any R&D at consortia will be larger, riskier, broader and more long-term than industry's R&D. Therefore, interviewees were asked to compare consortia with firms that do conduct R&D.

Although consortia programs are small, they perform a significant part of the R&D in many industries. Indeed, if it weren't for consortia, many industries would solely dependent on the R&D of suppliers.

Characteristics of Specific Projects: Any difference between consortia and member firms is significant for policy. On this point, there is a consensus in literature that consortia conduct different kinds of projects (Industrial Research Institute, 1975). Specifically, cooperative projects may be: 1) larger, 2) riskier, 3) more long-termed, and 4) more complex. The data in Tables 29 to 31 examine differences between consortia and industry with comparative data from actual projects in the textile, electric, and gas industries.[13]

---

[12] The agreement that consortia work is broader needs clarification. Some sources confused breadth with depth of focus. Industry was thought to employ professional generalists (e.g., electrical engineering) while consortia employed professionals with depth in specialties (e.g., circuit theory).

[13] Data were provided by the person most familiar with the R&D program since, for all characteristics except budgets, no data bases existed. In other words, the measures above are educated estimates.

Table 28

Opinions on Consortia vs. Corporate R&D Projects*

Characteristic	Textiles Consortia	Co.	Gas/Electric Consortia	Co.	Food Consortia
Larger	3.0	3.0	4.2	4.1	3.6
Riskier	2.7	3.2	3.8	3.5	3.4
Broader	4.0	3.1	3.9	3.9	4.0
Longer Horizon	1.2/5.0 **	3.6	4.1	3.5	3.1
Less Competitive	4.0	3.5	3.5	3.5	3.4
	(N=9)	(N=10)	(N=14)	(N=15)	(N=8)

* Data are from a Likert scale of 1 = Strongly Disagree to 5= Strongly Agree

**TRI and ITT differed were at opposite poles.

Table 29
Characteristics of Textile R&D Projects

ID	Characteristic	Companies			
		Consortia	Small	R&D+	All
A	Total Program Budget	$99,000	$2l3,000	$1,090,000	$691,000
B	Annual Budget	34,000		287,000	117,000
C	Probability of Tech Success	0.79	1.0	0.58	0.45
D	Prob. of Commercialization	0.81		0.60	.7.5
E	Prob. of Commercial Success	0.83		0.74	0.70
F	Overall Probability of Success	0.54	1.0	0.26	0.24
G	Breadth	2.6	1.0	3.4	2.6
H	Years to Commercial Success	1.3	2.0	3.0	2.9
I	Info vs. Hardware Output	1.9	4.0	7.0	6.1
J	State of Art Advance	NA	0.0	2.4	3.2
K	Relation to Other Work	2.3	1.0	2.2	2.4
L	% Basic Research	NA	0.0	3.0	2.1
M	%Applied Research	17.7	0.0	20.0	23.3
N	%Development	3.3	0.0	43.0	46.9
O	%Design	3.6	100.0	22.0	22.4
B	%Test Procedure	25.0	0.0	12.0	5.3
P	%Field Testing	48.4	0.0	-	-
		100%	100%	100%	100%
		(N=9)	(N=2)	(N=5)	(N=20)

Notes

"Total Program Budget" was for related projects over several years.

G: Measured by the number of technical fields involved in a project or program.

I: Information Output Only = 1.0; Hardware = 7.0 J: Effect on a Std. Text; 1 = No Impact, 5.0 = Major Impact.

K: 1 = Work significant on its own; 7 = Work is a small piece of an evolving field

L thru P: Type of Work (% of Total Effort);

R&D + = R&D Oriented Companies

Table 30

Characteristics of Electric Power R&D Projects

ID	Characteristic	Consortia	Companies R&D +	All
A	Total Program Budget	$2,192,000	$6,500,000	$2,763,000
B	Annual Budget	582,000	767,000	303,000
C	Probability of Tech Success	0.68	0.88	0.85
D	Prob. of Commercialization	0.91	0.83	0.75
E	Prob. of Commercial Success	0.76	1.00	0.86
F	Overall Probability of Success	0.47	0.73	0.54
G	Breadth	3.5	2.0	2.2
H	Years to Commercial Success	8.6	2.0	3.4
I	Info vs. Hardware Output	3.9	3.8	2.9
J	State of Art Advance	4.0	3.8	2.7
K	Relation to Other Work	2.5	1.3	2.4
L	% Basic Research	7.5	-	13.0
M	%Applied Research	48.5	-	18.0
N	%Development	14.5	30.0	16.0
O	%Design	4.0	70.0	45.0
B	%Test Procedure	25.5	-	8.0
P	%Field Testing	-	-	-
		100%	100%	100%
		(N=10)	(N=4)	(N=12)

Notes

(As for Table 29)

Table 31

Characteristics of Gas R&D Projects

ID	Characteristic	Companies Consortia	R&D +	All
A	Total Program Budget	$1,822,000	$330,000	$238,000
B	Annual Budget	244,000	94,000	71,000
C	Probability of Tech Success	0.51	0.58	0.67
D	Prob. of Commercialization	0.60	0.76	0.76
E	Prob. of Commercial Success	0.69	0.71	0.75
F	Overall Probability of Success	0.21	0.31	0.38
G	Breadth	2.7	1.5	1.6
H	Years to Commercial Success	6.5	7.1	7.1
I	Info vs. Hardware Output	4.2	6.3	5.7
J	State of Art Advance	4.0	3.0	2.6
K	Relation to Other Work	2.8	2.0	1.6
L	% Basic Research	28.9	11.3	-
M	% Applied Research	42.0	36.2	-
N	% Development	8.3	32.4	-
O	% Design	7.8	13.8	-
B	% Test Procedure	13.0	6.3	-
P	% Field Testing	-	-	-
		100%	100%	100%
		(N=8)	(N=4)	(N=7)

Notes

(As for Table 29)

Table 29 on textile consortia projects and shows them to be: 1) smaller, 2) less risky, 3) equally broad, 4) shorter in planning horizon, and 5) more information oriented. A mixed picture is found in the electric power industry (Table 30) where cooperative projects are smaller but more risky, broader, and longer-termed. Table 31 on gas industry projects presents consortia projects as: 1) much larger, 2) riskier, 3) broader, 4) equally long-term in planning horizon, and 5) slightly more likely to affect the state-of-the art.[14]

Comparison of the data on gas and electric projects shows that the former are not uniquely large, broader or longer-termed. It is possible that, once gas industry R&D grows, differences between consortia and corporate R&D will lessen. The higher risk of gas projects may also reflect a set of stronger consortia managers in that industry.[15] Managers of the newer gas consortia may see that power moderate as their organizations age.

Data from all three industries show less risk at consortia than in R&D intensive industries. Edwin Mansfield (1971) found that the average probabilities in those industries are: a) probability of technical success = 0.5, b) probability of commercialization given technical success=0.5 and, c) probability of commercial success given commercialization =0.4 or an overall probability of success of (.5 x .5 x .4) =0.1.

Consortia and Basic Research

Many sources believe consortia are well positioned to undertake basic research. They argue that, since basic research is risky, consortia are better suited for risk sharing. A second rationale is based on the observation that commercial exploitation of basic research is difficult. Since industries as a whole benefit from the research, consortia are believed to be better suited to undertake basic projects.

Prior research found that consortia have higher commitments to basic research than private firms. For example, Jones found that RA budgets for basic research are significantly higher than the industrial average (23% vs. 5%). Data was gathered in this study using the definition of basic research of the National Science Foundation:

> Original investigations for the advancement of scientific knowledge which
> do not have specific commercial objectives, although they may be in fields
> of present or potential interest to a given industry

Consortia commitments to basic research are both stronger (Table 32) than industry and held for longer periods of time. It is possible, however, that the strong

---

[14] All gas consortia were engaged in large, government sponsored projects. Therefore, the data in Table 31 are based on projects funded only with industrial funds.

[15] This is an oversimplification for the Electric Power Research Institute. At the time of this study, EPRI was building its staff. However most of its projects were inherited from the Edison Electric Institute which was strongly controlled by committees.

commitments in Table 32 reflect high commitments by a few consortia. Table 33 shows that approximately half of consortia programs have low involvement in basic research.

Data on specific projects at one consortium are worth reporting since it is famous for a strong commitment to basic research. Data on three of its basic research projects showed work that had:

a. Greater risk (an average probability of commercial success of.06),

b. Greater impact on the state-of-the-art (all required revised chapters), and

c. Definite ties to a stream of continuing research (an average score of 4.7)

Table 32

Commitment to Basic Research

Year	% of Budget in Basic Research
1970	22.7 %
1972	23.9 %
1974	23.4 %

Table 33

Variation in Commitments to Basic Research

Type of Program	N	% Basic Research
Solely in Basic Research	11	55.1
Basic Research + One Other Function	13	40.9
Basic Research + a Wide Variety of Functions	16	23.1
Emphasis on 1 or 2 Other Functions	41	3.9
	81	

The Value of Consortia

Member firms admire consortia competence but are disappointed in their contributions. For example, many executives could not think of one important consortium contribution; despite agreeing that a list of projects defined as important by their consortium were so. On the whole, members rated consortia output as comparable to "inputs of outside sources" such as literature, trade shows, and supplier contracts (Table 34). Table 35 lists specific benefits from the list of important projects.

Table 34

Evaluation of Consortia Contributions

Contributions	Average Rating
Association on Regulatory Projects of Consortia	
Number of Contributions (NC) = 2, Number of Evaluations (NE = 24)	3.9
Consortia Committed to Technology Evaluation	
(NC=4, NE=24)	3.6
Large Consortia are Necessary in Energy	
(NC=8, NE=4)	3.4
Rating of All Consortia Values	
(NC=33, NE=32)	3.1
Association with Consortia Labs Committed to Basic Research	
(NC=3, NE=13)	2.8
Consortia Labs with Government $ for Applied Research	
(NC=6, NE=8)	1.9

The scale rated importance relative to outside sources: 1= much lower than average, 2 = lower than average, 3 = average, 4 = greater than average and 5 =much greater than average

Table 35

Benefits of Consortia Membership*

Benefit	Food Consortia (N=8)	Textile Consortia (N=8)	Co. (N=8)	Electric/Gas Consortia (N=18)	Co. (N=20)
Original Knowledge	3.6	3.9	3.5	3.9	3.4
Improved Product Tech.	3.1	3.1	2.3	3.9	2.6
Improved Process Tech.	4.0	3.4	2.8	4.1	3.1
Report on Outside Tech.	3.5	4.1	3.6	4.0	2.9
Interpretative S&T	3.6	4.4	3.0	3.9	3.2
Advice on Problems	3.9	4.5	2.5	3.7	3.1
Status as an R&D Org.	3.6	3.3	2.5	3.7	3.1
Satisfaction	3.9	2.6	3.6	3.4	3.1
Interaction w/other Orgs.	3.8	4.2	3.9	4.0	3.9
Information on Problems	4.0	3.5	3.1	3.7	3.3
All Benefits	3.7	3.7	3.1	3.8	3.1

* Each benefit was rated on a five-point scale of value.

5 = Very High Value - The benefit obtained is essential to member and firm operations and the cost of the member reproducing the benefit on their own would clearly exceed the cost of membership.

4 = High Value - The benefit obtained while not essential is of clear value to member firms and if reproduced by them would clearly exceed the cost of membership.

3 = Moderate Value - The benefit obtained is of clear value, but could be reproduced by the member at a cost roughly equal to that of membership.

2 = Low Value - The benefit obtained is either of marginal value to the member or it could be reproduced at a cost lower than that of membership.

1 = No Value - Members receive no clear benefits of this kind.

** An approximate guide to statistical significance on the t test method is:

Sample Size	Difference for 10% Significance
10	0.6
20	0.4

Innovativeness vs. Involvement in Consortia: All sources rated the largest firms in their industry as high, moderate, or low on innovativeness and consortia staffs rated members on degree of involvement in the consortium. Table 36 examines the association between innovativeness and involvement. Students of cooperative organizations (Aiken and Rage) argue that the direction of causality in this association is not critical since the key is that innovative organizations value cooperative programs. Aiken and Rage argue that the process is circular: diversity of inputs breeds innovation, which breeds need for outside resources, which triggers consortia involvement, which leads to further diversity of inputs

Table 36

Innovativeness vs. Consortia Involvement

Textile Companies	Involvement*	# Members
Top 12 Innovative Co.	1.93	12
Bottom 12 Co.	1.06	6
Gas Companies		
Top 9 Innovative Co.	2.61	All are members
Bottom 9 Co.	1.56	
Electric Power Companies		
Top 9 Innovative Co.	2.61	All are members
Bottom 9 Co.	1.69	
Electric & Gas Companies		
Top 9 Innovative Co.	1.82	All are members
Bottom 9 Co.	1.11	

* Rated by consortia staffs on a scale of 1 = Low to 3 = High

Several studies of industrial innovation argue that innovative firms maintain many channels of communication. The importance of consortia as one such channel highlights both informal communications such as committee interaction and formal communications such as conferences, journals, and publications.

Value of Membership: Consortia managers' believed large, R&D intensive firms tended to obtain high value from membership. For example, 25 of 29 responses from energy consortia were the largest firms in the industry. Textile consortia listed seven large firms, two medium, and eight small firms. Executives at the Institute of Textile Technology were alone in listing the small firms they targeted in formal programs.

Staffs believe that large firms focus on improving technology and small on using technology. One executive of a small upholstery fabric firm said: "We aren't interested in improvements in what the big companies are doing. Our survival depends on finding a niche where they are not active."

However, almost all sources believed size is not a prerequisite for benefits. Seventy percent stressed full participation in consortium activities and active use of consortium services.[16] The following comments about high benefit firms are typical:

a. They serve on all the major committees and thus obtain both a voice in the work we undertake and get the know-how that never appears in reports.

b. They are committed to our success and fully support our work.

c. The key is active, personal contact between our staff and the companies. We continually hear from and visit with involved companies.

d. They react quickly when we offer something and have the competence to use our work. They are genuinely innovative in our industry.

e. They had the foresight to anticipate crises in the industry. Thus, we found they were already active on planned projects. They provide useful critiques of plans, knowledgeable advisors, and leverage their work with ours.

Role of Consortia in Textile Technology

Five consortia focused on textile technology; two had annual budgets greater than $300,000, and all had universally respected staffs. Sources especially valued contributions from these consortia on: a) education, b) technical information, c) technology use, and d) basic research.

Education: All textile consortia are active in continuing education, but the Institute of Textile Technology (ITT) and the Textile Research Institute (TRI) also list graduate education as a primary function. Both educational programs are small (e.g., ITT accepted 10 master's students per year and a doctoral candidate every other year). There is also widespread agreement that a TRI degree, bearing the status of Princeton University, is an elite textile doctorate.

---

[16] Fifteen percent of responses referred to economic benefits because the firm was a test site. The other 15% listed such benefits as obtaining graduates, consulting on problems, evaluation of capital plans, and comparative information about industry standing.

Similar, multi-disciplinary education programs are found in the gas (Institute of Gas Technology) and paper (Institute of Paper Chemistry) industries. Similarity between these programs is not surprising since executives at ITT and IGT stated that they used the Institute of Paper Chemistry as a model.

Information: Textile consortia play important roles in disseminating scientific and technological information. TRI published the leading, scientific journal in its field: The Textile Research Journal and ITT published the leading abstract journal: The Textile Technology Digest. ITT also developed a valued thesaurus for textile information systems.[17] Finally, all consortia are active in running conferences and seminars. Publication outlets originate virtually exclusively with consortia. However, almost no consortia were active in locating, reviewing, and interpreting contributions from other organizations or fields in reviews of trends and issues.

Technology Utilization: Textile machinery and chemical treatments are important technologies for textile industry suppliers. Advances, especially in other countries, have had a minor impact in the U.S. and this fact has led consortia to encourage greater attention to new technologies via tests at member mills including data on: costs of operation, skill requirements, operating issues, and output quality. These evaluations may accelerate diffusion and use of supplier innovations.

A similar situation exists for the raw materials used in textiles. From 1960 to 1972, U.S. annual synthetic fiber use rose from 28% to 64% and included continual improvements by chemical producers. Unlike machinery, however, fiber makers have greater market power than textile producers. The combined power of textile firms acting through a consortium substantially increased textiles power. In one case, mills experienced technical problems with a certain fiber and a member requested that their consortium do a study. The study showed the fiber was indeed a major problem and its supplier responded with corrective action.

All consortia were active in consulting on new technologies. However, consulting at all but one, the Institute of Textile Technology, had no formal programs for small companies. Each member of ITT is eligible for an annual audit of both wet (chemical and dyeing operations) and dry processes (carding, spinning and weaving). These audits completely review operations with data on inputs, outputs, quality, costs, and operating difficulties and recommend improvements in operations as well as on new technologies. Firms may use also 15% of membership dues targeted at specific operating issues and, on a typical day, half of ITT's staff is assigned to a member mill.

---

[17] The Encyclopedia of Information Services describes ITT's services as follows: "[It's] Computer file contains information from over 90,000 documents abstracted in the Textile Technology Digest. Library holdings are more than 20,000 books and bound periodicals, plus patents, reprints, and trade literature."

Role of Consortia in Energy Technology

The Institute of Gas Technology (IGT) is similar to ITT and TRI in that it also has both graduate and doctoral education programs. However, unlike TRI and ITT, IGT is a formal part of a university (Illinois Institute of Technology). Even though IGT does not publish a primary journal, it does publish an abstract service and three newsletters: a) Gas Supply Review, b) Gas Scope on specific projects, and c) International Gas Technology Highlights on international industry news.

Primary activities of Electric and Gas consortia include: a) Pilot Plant Operation and Design, b) Standardization studies, and c) Long-range Planning on technological opportunities.

Pilot Plants: Coal Gasification was an important technology in the 1970s. Domestic coal was plentiful but produced significant pollution. Converting low-energy 'dirty' coal to high-energy, 'clean' gas was an attractive technology. Exploratory R&D on coal gasification was performed in the early 1970s. What remained were design, construction, and experimentation with large pilot plants to determine effectiveness and economics. Construction of such plants is a classic case of consortium justification since a pilot exceeded the resources of any one firm and no single company could use or promote a gas generation technology. Funding a pilot plant was only possible after Federal funding became available. Funds from the American Gas Association eventually made up one-third of the total with the other two thirds coming from the U.S. Office of Coal Research and later from the Energy Research and Development Agency (ERDA).

Standards: Most consortia are active on standardization.[18] Standardization affects the rate of innovation, the impact of technology, and the climate for innovation. An example is leakage from gas pipelines. Corroded pipes are dangerous and costly leakage must be found before explosive concentrations accumulate. Pin-pointing the location of leaks is costly and difficult with no clues beyond a gross discrepancy between usage and input. Once found, repairing leakages is expensive as it involves removal of old pipe and replacement with new material.

Advances in plastic sleeve technology offered one solution but at a high cost since a variety of plastics and pipe fittings were involved. Work would also be inefficient if every company had different pipes for different terrains, gas compositions, and system conditions. Individual effort would duplicate work, entail excessive inventory costs, and lead to short production runs. Gas companies understood the situation and supported a standardization program by the American Gas Association (AGA) at Battelle Institute that is widely regarded as a highly valuable contribution of the AGA.

Technological Planning: Only the American Gas Association (AGA) and the predecessor of EPRI (the Electric Research Council or ERC) conduct formal programs of

---

[18] Standardization was once was a common function of consortia. But an antitrust ruling restricted it to utilities.

long-range R&D planning.[19] Both programs: a) define needs for R&D; b) locate, assess and match technologies to needs; and c) project resource and action needs. Each program produces a formal report to industry and to interested outsiders.

Both AGA and ERC – EPRI rely on expert judgment and consensus to: a) choose major areas of work (such as technologies for power generation); and b) consult with industry on needs, opportunities, and resource requirements. Consortia staff analyzes the data and a Coordinating Panel assembles program plans.

This approach to planning undoubtedly is useful, but it is conservative and focused on existing technology. Further weaknesses of the process are:

a. Expertise is anchored in existing areas of science and technology,

b. Analyses are hierarchical breakdowns of existing technology,

c. Little systematic consideration is made of alternative technologies,

d. Exploratory science and alternative technologies are not sought,

e. Industry representatives are reluctant to obsolete existing technologies or to consider large investments,

f. Weak representation from social and economic interests results in linear projections of technology and action, and

g. Views of consumer and public interests are not sought.

In short, reliance on the judgment and consensus of stakeholders is likely to yield incremental plans that fail to produce innovation. This weakness may not be crucial if existing technology adequately satisfies society's needs. When innovation is required, however, different approaches to planning are called for (Chapter 4).

Opinions of Government Policy

Could government policy create incentives to consortia innovation? To elicit answers, executives of both consortia and industrial firms were asked the following question:

> The U.S. is unique in its lack of governmental support for R&D consortia. In most European countries, cooperative R&D is encouraged via direct grants, favorable legislation, governmental services etc. Accordingly, sources were asked to indicate the extent to which several government actions would enhance the contribution of consortia to progress.

Two caveats are needed. It was necessary to compare U.S. to European policy because most sources gave little thought to policy changes.   Indeed, many sources found it difficult to believe government could effectively administer any positive action. Possible government actions had to be rated as if ideally administered.   Sources expected only moderate improvements from U. S. government changes (Table 37) and

---

[19] The ERC was an intermediate organization in the history electric power R&D. This history began with the Edison Electric Institute and progressed to the Electric Power Research Institute (EPRI) in the 1970s.

could not name a project, technology, or piece of useful knowledge that might result from government support. Instead, sources stayed with generalities about 'better' or 'more innovative' work or 'doing more of what we already do'.

The most favored action was grants for specific technologies already in existence. Thirty-one percent of respondents received government grants and 47% participated in joint projects with government. Even though grants were already in use, many respondents wished to reduce: red tape and perceived 'unfairness in government handling." Eleven respondents rated improvement of contract procedures as a significant inducement to greater productivity. Sources also had qualifications about the second highest item; unrestricted grants. Many expressed doubts about how "unrestricted" grants could be and felt that any government involvement in programs would hinder consortia. Simply put, all preferred consortia to be left alone. This attitude also appeared in the Battelle (1956, p. 28) survey:

> "...Federal legislation, regulations, and agencies apparently have little or no effect on cooperative research. Antirust actions at one time a popular 'bug-a-boo' of trade associations seem a thing of the past ... If any feeling at all is projected it is that minimum governmental regulation and supervision is desired."

Negative views about government should not be overemphasized. When pressed for specifics about government hindrances, sources could not support their opinions with facts or examples. Many consortia also claimed "valuable" relationships with specific agencies. In other words, the negative tone reflected adversary relationships on taxes, antitrust oversight, or environmental regulation. Indeed, friction was especially noted at trade associations that are active in lobbying government.

This study concludes that consortia are not brimming with ideas for technologies that await enlightened government action. However, this does not mean there is no role for government; just that productive actions have to be identified by government itself, promoted by government, and nurtured long enough to provide a fair trial.

Table 37

Opinions on the Impact of Government Actions*

Gov. Action	All Cons. (N=30)	Co, (N=17)	Textile Cons. (N=10)	Co. (N=7)	Electric/Gas Cons. (N=12)	Co, (N=10)	Food Cons. (N=8)
Broad Contracts	3.6	3.6	3.0	3.7	4.1	3.4	3.8
Unrestricted $	3.8	3.4	3.6	3.1	3.9	2.4	3.9
Tech Adoption $	3.4	2.5	3.0	2.5	4.0	2.6	3.1
Regulation $	3.1	2.5	3.3	3.0	3.0	2.2	3.1
New Consortia	2.8	2.4	2.6	2.7	2.8	2.2	3.0
Antitrust Change	2.0	1.8	1.7	1.2	1.6	2.1	2.8
Taxation Change	1.4	1.4	1.0	1.0	1.7	1.8	1.5

* The Scale was: 1 = no improvement to 5 = great improvement

Significance: t test 10% significance if differences are 0.6 or greater (N=10), 0.5 (N=15), and 0.4 (N=20)

Summary

Few consortia projects make direct contributions to innovation and fewer still pioneer new technologies. Instead, the projects of consortia make indirect contributions to such activities as: a) fundamental research, b) improvements in materials and processes, c) consulting on technical operations, d) standards and testing technology, and e) assistance in technology transfer. Members believe that these benefits provide an adequate return on membership fees and that consortia are staffed by dedicated and competent professionals.

Simply put, cooperation is difficult; especially cooperative innovation. A fundamental characteristic of innovation is that it is a process of departure from existing thinking, that is, innovation is accompanied by: a) lack of common language, b) difficulty on proprietary information, c) absence of entrepreneurial personalities, and d) difficulty winning consensus. In short, this study concludes that government cannot rely on consortia to work at variance with their nature. Consortia themselves must find value in innovative work that is consistent with their nature.

Chapter 4

THE POTENTIAL OF CONSORTIA

"Sure, our industry's venture in cooperative R&D didn't amount to much. But I hope we are not judged on that. There is a lot of potential in cooperation and it is on this potential that government and the industry must focus." (Survey Respondent)

Government support for consortia would be reasonable if they made significant contributions to technical progress. But all studies show that, though worthwhile, consortia contributions are not significant. U.S. Members and consortia also believe there is no need for government support. In fact, several make it clear they would not welcome support.

If output and opinion were sole guides, the message would be: government should do little or nothing. However, the potential of consortia in underactive areas is significant including in: (1) technological planning, (2) technology transfer and utilization, (3) regulatory strategy, and (4) basic research. Special consideration is also warranted on the role of consortia in non-competitive industries.

R&D Contractors and Consortia Laboratories

This study differentiates 1) consortia that contract out R&D and 2) consortia that operate laboratories. The operations of Contractors do not warrant new government support. However, much of the unrecognized value of consortia requires the in-depth expertise of Labs. Most Laboratories operate sophisticated programs staffed by professionals who have continuity of hands-on expertise and contacts. These assets call for consideration of potential contributions to national innovation.

Table 38 lists the Consortia Laboratories in this survey. The median R&D budget for Laboratories was $265,000 and all consortia with budgets over $5 million operated laboratories. The staffs of Laboratories originate projects (Table 39), play central roles in project management and interpretation, and capitalize on locations near universities (Table 40).

Table 38

U. S. Consortia Laboratories*

(*Asterisks = professionals on the staff: * 1-10 professionals, ** 11-20, and *** 21 or more.)

SIC Industry

Agriculture	*** Cotton Inc.
12 Coal Mining	*** Bituminous Coal Research
20 Foods	* American Inst. of Baking; Int'l Sugar Research Fnd.
	* Dried Fruit Assoc. of CA; *** National Canners Assoc.
22 Textiles	*** Textile Res. Institute; *** Inst. of Textile Technology
	* International Fabricare Institute
24 Lumber & Wood	* Hardwood Plywood Manufacturing Assoc.;
	*** Plywood Research Fnd. * American Pulpwood Assoc.
26 Paper	*** Institute of Paper Chemistry
	** National Council of the Paper Industry
27 Printing & Publishing	** American Newspaper Publishing Association
	** Graphic Arts Technical Fnd. * Graphic Arts Research Fnd.
	* Gravure Research Institute
28 Chemicals	(Textile Research Institute – Fiber Program)
29 Petroleum	* Asphalt Institute
31 Leather	* Tanner's Council of America
32 Stone Clay& Glass	* National Crushed Stone Assoc. Cement & Concrete Res. Inst.
	Brick Institute of America; * National Sand & Gravel Assoc.
	National Claypipe Institute; ** Tile Council of America
34 Fabricated Metals	* Cast Iron Pipe Institute
39 Miscellaneous Manufacturing	Gemological Institute of America
Railroads	American Association of Railroads
Airlines	Flight Safety Foundation
Construction Services	* National Concrete Masonry Association
	* Steel Structure Painting Council
49 Gas & Electric	*American Gas Association; *** Institute of Gas Technology
	*** Electric Power Research Institute
Miscellaneous	*Lawn Institute

Table 39

Origin of Consortia Laboratory Projects

Primary Origin	% Labs
Consortia Staff	79
Member Reps.	8
Other	13
	100.0%
	(N = 24)

Table 40

Location of Consortia Laboratories

Located Near a University	N	%
Yes	19	70
No	8	30
	(N=27)	100%

Located Near Consortia Industry	N	%
Yes	15	58
No	11	42
	(N=26)	100%

Laboratories and Technology Planning

The two most commonly studied types of innovation are: (1) incremental improvement of existing technology and (2) radical departure to a new technology (Utterback; Kelly, Kranzberg, et al; and Zaltman, Duncan and Holbek). Progress in incremental innovation centers on corporate laboratories that enhance existing products and processes. These, laboratories develop improvements some of which even accumulate into major progress (Enos). This study shows that consortia complement industry generated improvements with studies providing depth on commonly used materials and processes.

Work on radical innovations is rare at consortia[20] since they originate in new industries, start small, and grow into new market segments (Cooper). A classic sequence occurred in communications: organized mail to telegraph, to telephone, to radio, etc. An important type of radical innovation is a major departure requiring extensive resources such as for shale oil, deep-sea mining, and fuel cell technologies. Opportunities for such large and radical innovations often build on convergences of existing technology. (Hochmuth) One example is convergence of streamlining, radial engine, and aerodynamics (ex. retractable landing gear) into the DC-3. Consortia Laboratories could be positioned to anticipate needs and opportunities for convergence and to perform supporting R&D. A prerequisite for Laboratory contributions on radical convergences is experience in technology planning and strategic thinking about new systems.

Radical innovations may restructure industries or create new industries. An example would be a switch on apparel from the system of shuttling – weaving – cutting – and sewing to blow molding fibers into garments. No one company could afford to work on blow molded apparel without new knowledge of prerequisites for comfortable, shape-holding, and durable garments. Research generating such knowledge could be an attractive focus for Consortia Labs. Other opportunities for restructuring systems include: 1) reducing the stages of common processes (Direct Reduction of Metals and Decentralized Electricity Transmission), 2) overcoming natural obstacles (Thin Seam Mining), and 3) automating human performance (Pilotless Aircraft), and 4) opening existing systems to new technologies.

Laboratories and Technology Utilization

Consortia Laboratory programs on technology utilization can be especially valuable for smaller firms. R&D is costly and requires a critical mass of activity that only larger firms can afford. Smaller firms may overcome this limitation with the outputs of consortia (Jones and Johnson).

The work of the Institute of Textile Technology specializes in technology utilization with programs of continuing education on new technical developments.

- a. Technical audits and consulting about new and existing technology,
- b. Testing and validation of quality management at firms,
- c. Evaluation of materials and processes with advice on new developments,
- d. Interpretation of regulations and recommendations for action, and
- e. Information services targeted to needs of small companies.

---

[20] A major involvement of consortia in radical innovation occurred on type-setting in the publishing industry. Printing machine users formed a consortium when they believed machine producers were not pursuing radical new technologies that involve photography (Bright).

Laboratories and the Regulatory Process

Many consortia had strong programs on technology issues involved in government regulations. These issues included the impact of:

a. Production processes on the environment (paper production's influence on water and air quality),

b. Product use on consumer health and safety (side effects of cosmetic ingredients and flame retardant clothing), and

c. Production work on employee health and safety (cotton dust).

Tables 26 and 27 (on pages 37 and 38) show that regulatory work makes up a third of the average consortium's program. Projects focused on improving environmental or health/safety technology was roughly 20% of all projects, and projects focused on regulation standards made up an additional 13%. Consortia services such as testing, consulting, and equipment evaluation also assist firms to interpret and conform to regulations. One such service was described as follows:

> "An Environmental Technical Information Center" (ETIC) handles information on ... the protection and utilization of environmental resources through R&D on byproduct recovery and effluent treatment, biological monitoring of effluent effects, predicting and correlating environmental responses through mathematical models and experimental measurements, and retrieval and critical analysis of technical information."

Consortia work on regulatory matters involves two managerial processes; 1) a dialectic process, where industry uses Labs to address regulation, and 2) a cooperative process on government and industry's joint interest in regulatory R&D. Despite their promise, both processes are complex in application and require further research.

The Dialectic Process: The dialectic process (Churchman, 1971) commonly occurs with new or expanded standards. Industry may feel there is inadequate knowledge and time for expanded regulation. Some firms may also prefer standards close to current practice that raise no new problems. Governmental expansion of standards is less adversarial if an industry has an active and respected consortium. Government and the consortium may negotiate on R&D and current practice as well as the potential of new technologies. This process of challenge, negotiation, consortium study, and joint resolution was observed in several industries.

An issue of fiber flammability received significant publicity regarding the safety of children's sleepwear. In response to public concern, government developed standards for fabric flammability that the industry labeled "disastrous" because it felt no known fabric could meet the proposed standards' at an acceptable cost. Indeed. The American Apparel Manufacturers Association (AAMA) responded with a study of burning injuries it hoped would deter proposed standards.

Proposed standards centered on: 1) the rate of garment consumption, and 2) the amount of molten drip. Industry focused on molten drip, because most garments were entirely synthetic (dacron, nylon, rayon, etc.) or a mix of natural and synthetic fibers. Synthetic fibers also provided texture sought by the market and were less expensive. The AAMA surveyed doctors to obtain data on molten drip. The results argued that the most important factor in injuries was garment flames rather than molten drip. This result motivated government to drop molten drip standards.

Public outcry motivated government to issue new standards. The textile and apparel industries responded with research at the Textile Research Institute (TRI) and the AAMA. Industry's case was strengthened when TRI developed a test procedure showing that garment construction had a substantial impact on flammability. Additional research supported came from both the National Bureau of Standards and the Man-Made Fibers Producers Association.

The Cooperative Process: Consortia use contacts to facilitate implementation and have hands-on familiarity with conditions impacting regulation. Finally, staffs possess the reputations valued by government and public advocates. Table 41 presents data from all consortia that show a reliance on Environmental Protection Agency (EPA) funding.[21] A similar picture appears in Table 42 on shared consortia and government projects and in Table 43 on grants from consortia.

Complexities of Practice: No trend was found in government sponsored R&D at consortia. There was a tendency for new consortia to focus on regulatory matters (ten of 19 new programs). However, expenditures on government-consortia cooperation did not grow over five years. Indeed, several prominent programs decreased. Of fifteen programs with $100,000/year budgets, eight had zero or negative growth and seven had positive growth. Of four programs with budgets greater than $1 million/year, three had negative growth on regulatory R&D and only one increased.

Interviews at eleven consortia with budgets of $100,000 per year illustrated the complexities in industry-government interaction that discouraged budget growth at consortia and sometimes discouraged government agencies. Three issues stood out:

a. Discussions were not based on science but focused on political, economic, social issues, and involved trade-offs on energy consumption.

b. Shared understanding of history was sometimes absent and skewed interaction away from shared interests and needs.[22]

c. Mutual respect and trust was difficult.

---

[21] Interviews showed that many contracts were not for R&D as usually understood. Technical work was present, but many EPA, NSF, and ERDA contracts emphasized data gathering on current practice.

[22] One article on noise regulations noted that Congress failed "to accept the fact that the years of instant environmental regulation ... are gone,' says Charles Elkins, EPA's assistant administrator for noise control."

Table 41

Government Contract & Grants *

Contractors That	N	%
Received No Contracts or Grants	37	51
Engaged in Shared Funding Only	19	26
Received Contracts or Grants From:		
One Agency	13	18
Two Agencies	3	4
Three Agencies	0	0
Four or More Agencies	1	1
	73	100%

Contractor or Grant Agency	N	%
Environmental Protection Agency	12	71
National Science Foundation	3	18
Energy R&D Agency	2	12
Forest Service	1	6
Department of Labor	1	6
Air Force	1	6
Army	1	6
Navy	1	6
Federal Aviation Authority	1	6
	23	100%

* Only includes data from Contractor Consortia. See Chapter 5 for data on Consortia Labs.

** Four contractors received support from more than one agency.

Table 42

Consortia & Government R&D Sharing

Agency Shared With	# Consortia
Environmental Protection Agency	14
OSHA	1
Department of Agriculture	13
Forest Products Laboratory	4
National Bureau of Standards	10
Department of Transportation	7
Bureau of Public Roads	3
Department of Interior	1
Bureau of Mines	2
Office of Coal Research	2
U.S. Navy	2
U.S. Army	1
Corp of Engineers	1
Dep't. of Housing & Urban Dev.	2
National Science Foundation	2
Energy R&D Agency	2
Federal Energy Authority	1
Atomic Energy Commission	1
Tennessee Valley Authority	1
Nuclear Regulatory Commission	1
Federal Power Commission	1
Health, Education, & Welfare	1
National Institute of Health	1

Table 43
Contracts and Grants to Government from Consortia

Industrial Consortia (N = 16)	**# Consortia**	**%**
National Bureau of Standards	8	50
Bureau of Mines	4	25
Forest Products Laboratory	3	19
U.S. Department of Agriculture	3	19
Argonne National Laboratory	2	13
Brookhaven National Laboratory	1	6
Oakridge National Laboratory	1	6
Tennessee Valley Authority	1	6
Environmental Protection Agency	1	6
Agricultural Consortia (N = 5)		
U.S. Department of Agriculture	5	100

Many sources in industry and consortia believe R&D by consortia has little or no impact on government policymakers:

a. "Government wants arm's-length confrontation on recommendations and suspects industry even though their technical people don't. The problem is different interpretations not validity. Some feel only universities can produce good R&D."

b. "Government and industry must agree on facts; understanding that these may be interpreted in different ways by different scientists and officials."

c. "Government decision makers don't understand priorities for action. A whole slew of regulations are eroding our industry. They have deflected us by requiring money to be spent in wrong areas and this discredits the feds."

d. The problem is the proliferation and lack of foresight in regulations. How can you do R&D if there is no logic to regulations?"

e. "We have a counter-productive 'technology-forcing, regulatory program'. It diminishes enthusiasm for new tools when current tools are mandated across the board, regardless of need. Why should industry develop new tools if they will be told to use them everywhere, indiscriminately?"

f. "Although environmental work has declined, work on safety has increased. We continue to gear up on safety, despite OSHA, because it is an inherent concern. Our interest in safety is apart from regulations; it is an interest stemming from public use of our service and employee interest in safety."

Other consortia welcome government sharing of funding and planning especially tripartite interpretations with government, industry, and academia. However, no consortium has an administrative structure for tripartite arrangements. The willingness is there and that willingness invites research and managerial experimentation.

Consortia Laboratories and Basic Research

The contributions of consortia to basic research contradict fears about a decline of industrial support that many believe threatens the productivity of R&D in the U.S.[23]

The Scale of Basic Research: Eleven consortia with budgets greater than $15,000/year said they devoted at least 50% of their budgets to basic research.[24] Interviews with directors qualified this finding by noting that member firms are becoming disenchanted with basic research as a primary function. Table 44 shows that as many Labs are seeing increased basic research as are seeing it decline.

One consortium that increased basic total R&D was active in energy where new demands were pushing the industry into new research. Another growing program was in a service industry that was vulnerable to public pressure on consumer health and safety. Several organizations with decreasing support for basic research noted that members were pressing for "more relevant" R&D and more "applications of basic research".

Basic Research as a Collective Good: Some consortia experienced a misunderstanding on basic research as collective benefits. When properly applied, the theory requires that research findings be translated into participatory benefits that are useful to members. In other words, basic knowledge must lead to private benefits for members not just to publications. Scientists at consortia will find that such participatory benefits emerge from the cumulative force of several studies which means that consortia require competence in locating, interpreting, and deriving useful knowledge.

---

[23] This study used the definition of basic research of the National Science Foundation: "Original investigations for the advancement of scientific knowledge which do not have specific commercial objectives, although they may be in fields of present or potential interest to a given industry."

[24] Two consortia had R&D budgets in excess of $1,000,000/year and two had budgets greater than $300,000/year.   Others were in the $100-200,000/year range. The commitments of these organizations to basic research was paralleled by reliance on universities for contract research (i.e., the average portion of the budget spent at universities was 57.5% versus a 28.6% allocation for the rest of the sample).

Table 44

Basic Research Trends

# Consortia	Basic Res Trend	R&D $ Trend
2	Increase	Increase
1	Increase	Decrease
2	Stable	Stable
3	Decrease	Increase
1	Decrease	Decrease

(N = 7)

Opportunities for new science emerge when tech planning discloses possibilities for fundamental changes in technology such as previously cited examples that eliminate stages of production (Direct Reduction and Blow Molding). The basic research needed to develop this new knowledge and expertise will be useful in:

a. Assessing the feasibility of approaches (ex: laser vs. tokamak in fusion power)

b. Predicting environmental impact (ex: ultra-high voltage transmission systems)

c. Defining possible precedents of new technologies (ex: new fiber structures)

d. Interpreting university science (ex: research on fabric flammability)

e. Planning applied research on commercial issues (ex: fuel cells), and

f. Defining applied projects for members to conduct (ex: fiber reclamation).

Without knowledge generated by exploratory research, technological planning is mere cataloging of possibilities. With such knowledge and expertise, tech planning becomes a dynamic, evaluative, and creative process. In short, exploratory research and technological planning develop a symbiotic relationship that relies on research to explore and to clarify fundamental alternatives.

Basic research that systematizes knowledge of existing technologies can also produce By-product benefits for members.

a. Systematic trial and error may provide a basis for deductions about future improvements as when experiments on cellulose fiber reactivity produced basic understanding of wash and wear properties.

b. The cumulative body of technical data may be used to design materials and equipment such as for the projected physical-chemical characteristics of liquid gas mixtures under cryogenic conditions.

c. Solutions to specific problems may be generalized to a class of solutions such as theories of the diffusion of gases did for dense materials used in under-ground storage.

d. Work on the impacts of technology on environment, consumer health, and worker safety, may trigger ideas for regulatory improvements such as on the effects of aerosol technology on tobacco products.

Even when basic research is productive, government aid may not be warranted. The considerable task of obtaining private benefits from research could require expertise limited to large firms. If so, government could find itself in the position of supporting larger versus smaller firms.[25] Indeed, this effect was a factor in attacks on aid to English RAs (Johnson). Government might ameliorate this criticism by requiring a knowledge dissemination program for firms of all sizes.

In conclusion, consortia in general, and especially Consortia Labs, possess a valuable capability for basic research. However, that capability must be managed and augmented with knowledge utilization programs.

Consortia Laboratories and Universities: Are there differences between research at consortia and the traditional bastion of research at universities? Many sources believe the answer is no and that basic research at consortia is similar to that of universities.   Both institutions are believed to be capable in both theory and experimentation and both are believed to emphasize applicable basic research. Just as consortia must satisfy member firms, universities must satisfy grant sources as well as firms that hire students and faculty as consultants. One dean noted:

"Left to their own devices, faculty members would do little mission-oriented research; non-applicable basic research would be the rule. But for ten years, we've had state supported R&D and had to tell faculty we could lose this money if there was nothing to show for it. Now we've gradually seen more timely studies."

There was some agreement at both consortia and universities that the former are better positioned to conduct large and long-term programs requiring groups of professionals. For example, one consortium researcher noted:

"Universities are more application oriented in their basic research. They tend to obtain money for small scale, specific grants that are mission oriented.   We feel we need at least $40,000 for a program, whereas universities can get by with $5,000 and student help. Universities are unlikely to work on projects requiring the work of 3-4 professionals over a few years. They have no capability for coordination and continuity whereas these are strengths of our work."

_____

[25] The president of one consortium confirmed this by noting his organization only recruited staff from firms with substantial R&D programs of their own.

Sources also believed universities emphasize research by individuals. One dean noted: "There is little tendency to collaborate in universities." Yet such differences should not be stressed since universities are successful winning large government contracts for R&D that leads to programs of substantial size and length.

Some consortia leaders feel their organizations have closer ties to industry than universities and that advisory and oversight committees give consortia greater knowledge of practical problems and constraints. Other sources emphasized the direct interactions between universities and industry. Unfortunately, no sources in either industry or universities mentioned consortia as bridges between those two institutions.

In conclusion, it is apparent that institutional assessment requires case-by-case analysis. In this sense, universities and consortia are in competition for R&D support as well as in continuing education. Given such competition, it is important that sources not exhibit competitive attitudes that impair relations between them. Fortunately, this survey found general mutual respect that is proper for competent colleagues.

Government and Consortia in Noncompetitive Industries

To this point, the discussion has focused on industries where competition motivates R&D and on how consortia complement competitive R&D. This section focuses on industries where competition doesn't require R&D such as gas and electric utilities. Most of the prior discussion is applicable especially that on consortia management, technology planning, and basic research. The major point of difference concerns the institutional structure for R&D.

Traditionally, noncompetitive industries rely on supplier innovation such as on suppliers of electric power generators to utilities. Some sources questioned if suppliers adequately cover the needs of their industries. For example, suppliers may focus on improving technologies they sell and have little incentive to explore alternative technologies. In other words, noncompetitive industries may benefit from organizations that explore innovative technologies.

Two interesting structures for consortia in noncompetitive industries are: 1) compulsory consortia such as Cotton Inc. and 2) consortia stimulated with government funding such as the Electric Power Research Institute. Cotton, Inc. grew from the benefits many cotton farmers could see from R&D that helped cotton respond to the sharp inroads synthetic fibers into apparel markets. These farmers felt at the mercy of chemical firms spending hundreds of millions on R&D on new fibers.[26] The federal government responded by organizing a plebiscite in which farmers voted on an assessment for an R&D and marketing consortium. The enabling legislation provided that, if a majority of farmers approved the consortium, assessments would be mandatory for all.

---

[26] R&D was being performed at the laboratories of the U.S. Department of Agriculture (USDA). However, the work was not viewed as the aggressive program R&D farmers needed for competition.

Cotton farmers approved and the USDA established an organization to collect a tax to fund the organization.[27] The proceeds went to Cotton Inc. which has worked exclusively on cotton R&D and its marketing. USDA reviews assure that Cotton Inc.'s work complements rather than duplicates that of USDA laboratories.[28]

Government also played a role in the birth of the Electric Power Research Institute (EPRI)[29] ; a voluntary consortium that includes government utilities such as the Tennessee Valley Authority. These agencies have equal status in EPRI and pay the same fees based on electric power production. Their membership makes sure that government positions are represented on both R&D and new technology use.

Consortia in noncompetitive industries are an attractive way to pursue R&D within a free enterprise system. However, these consortia have only been formed after threat arose to the industry. Non-competitive industries, such as water that have had no threat have yet to consider cooperative R&D. The role of the federal government in stimulating cooperative programs in such industries and in changing the mix of government/supplier/cooperative R&D are important subjects for future exploration.

Summary

Technological innovation in the United States must be based on more than accident. A system is needed to generate the knowledge, resources, and work of innovation. Although much of that system exists; it is incomplete. America's system is excellent for improvements in existing technology and for using such technology in practice. The system is also productive in generating radical innovations with moderate capital requirements. But the system provides no way of anticipating the limits of existing technology or of generating alternatives that restructure industries. The system fails to provide the foresight, understanding, and new knowledge required for the commitment of the substantial resources needed to restructure technology. The system further fails to provide ways for new technology to be transferred between fields and for small organizations to maintain technological parity.

The programs of Consortia Laboratories must be expanded if they are to assume a role in the envisioned system. Especially important in this expansion would be managerial action to improve the effectiveness and efficiency of consortia operations and assure their organizational independence. The need for such improvements is the focus of the next chapter.

---

[27] The tax of $1/bale was collected at cotton gins. Gins were used for this purpose because there were few of them.   Some industries have been interested in their own versions of Cotton Inc., but have been stymied by the absence of an efficient way to collect a production tax.

[28] Similar programs were initiated for the beef, egg, and potato industries.

[29] Soon after EPRI's organization, its membership accounted for over 80% of electric power generated in the U.S. EPRI's budget for R&D became greater than all other U.S. consortia combined.

Chapter 5

THE PROMISE OF CONSORTIA LABORATORIES

"If results be the standard, the institutions of American ... technical change have been remarkably effective. They have been so because the inherent abilities of a profit oriented economy have been supplemented by government policies where private market incentives alone were not adequate to achieve satisfactory results. (Nelson, et al., p.171)

Many feel the American system for innovation is incomplete (Business Week, 1976) and, per Nelson, Peck, and Kalachek, believe improvement requires government support. This book argues that Consortia Laboratories could be a cornerstone of enhanced innovation in the United States. However, signs of managerial weakness at consortia abound. Instead of recognizing that management of collaboration is challenging, consortia underestimate its difficulty and shackle their organizations in administrative and technical detail. The result is weak programs and weak relations with members.

The typical program focuses on extensions of existing knowledge on known problems rather than results that challenge their industries. Why? Consortia managers and staffs take justifiable pride in their technical competence. If competence is not a problem, what is? One answer is openness to improving consortia management coupled with a will to build the training and systems needed for improvement.

Consortia management involves many of the most challenging tasks of management: inter-organizational decision making, communications spanning backgrounds, conflict resolution, and committee action on strategy, management through persuasion rather than authority, and marketing intangible benefits.[30] Like other R&D organizations, consortia must also cope with: resistance to change, venture management under uncertainty, motivating professional personnel, and assessing risk.

---

[30] A member of England's Parliament (Woodward, p. 39) cited Samuel Johnson, noted: ""Sir, running a Research Association is like a dog's walking on his hind legs. It is not done well, but one is surprised to find it done at all."

The relevant principles needed to address these issues are not obvious and some run counter to common sense. The following sections discuss such principles starting with those concerning cooperation of lab professionals and members focused on commercialization.

Principles of Collaborative Innovation

The following scenario is typical and illustrates the challenge of collaborative innovation.

> "Alice Sci's project was a big success! It produced unexpected findings that would yield a nice paper in a leading journal. Alice also looked forward to the attention and status her lab would receive in professional circles. Helen App even visited from HQ with welcome congratulations, but also claimed the project had applications that would yield significant gains for members. Helen was followed by a Patent Attorney, an Industrial Standards Specialist, a Manufacturing Engineer, and a Tech Writer for trade pubs. All these visitors took Alice's time and energy from paper writing, planning theoretical extensions, and visiting her academic mentor on scientific implications.
>
> What seemed straight forward became complicated as new people introduced new variables and demands for data on differently scaled conditions. Constraints on costs, regulations, and competitive conditions exacerbated the situation further. To make matters worse, Alice's inexperience in field testing led to that issue being assigned to engineers with little time to consult with the lab.

This example illustrates the challenge of collaborative innovation and the importance of training in its principles.

Agenda Control: Every cooperating party needs explicit and declared goals. Alice needs to decide what is most important for stage of research; gathering data or theoretical development of findings. The point person for commercialization needs to decide what is important for development; application data, or prototypes or economics and regulatory conformance. Without focused goals, cooperative progress will not be made. Each party will just switch attention to a target of the moment.

End Use Targeting: Each party must formulate their agenda in terms of how progress will benefit member firms and the customers they serve. Alice's quest for new knowledge must target phenomena and properties that occur in member processes and customer use. Helen's quest for applications must specify target markets and competitive contexts. Without End Use targeting, parties lack a jointly held focus.

Cross Systems Communication: The third principle calls on each party to formulate the other's agenda in their language. Suppose Helen needs to see if a phenomenon is feasible in a market context. Alice has to accept Helen's goal and express it in scientific terms. Suppose Alice's requires data on new variables and ranges. Helen must relate Alice's variables to commercial contexts. Both must be open to negotiate data and contexts to satisfy other's goals. In short, each party must understand the others' goals sufficiently to relate them to their own work.

70

This skill of understanding other's goals in both your and their languages requires substantial training and mentors who are able to not only explain but have the skills themselves. When achieved, the payoff is not only mutual respect but discovery of both new science and new applications not previously imagined.

Life Cycle Commitment: A basic characteristic of innovations is that they don't work according to prior plans. Spectacular failures are more common than successes (Cooper and Schendel). That being the case, the support of top management and the enduring commitment of professionals and commercial experts is crucial. This need for reinforced trust is so basic that common commitment must be accompanied by life-cycle, on-site interaction at each stage of the innovation process.

Principles of Consortia Organization

Managerial weaknesses are especially apparent on cooperative communication, decision making, and change as illustrated in the common examples of weaknesses below.

    a. Biannual meetings on one-day reviews of project status and of agendas focused on reacquainting members with each other and lab program.

    b. Piles of R&D proposals sent to committees without summaries or structure so that member representatives end up reading while traveling.

    c. Meetings held without staff work on plans, issues, and conflicts while staffs focus on administrative and technical detail.

    d. Committee members accepted from companies without vetting, guidance, or recruitment criteria defining needed expertise and mission.[31]

    e. Simple progress reviews with no policy overview.

    f. Technical reports limited to laboratory work with no context of industrial forces, university science, and external discoveries.

Signs of disorganization do not imply incompetence or lack of dedication. But, consortia need to complement technical direction with attention to managerial issues that may contradict the assumptions of technical direction.[32] Contradictory as the following may sound, consortia managers must be ready to: disagree with members on the industry's best interests, limit the size of membership, commit funds to ideas before member approval, and limit activities that build consortia prestige.

---

[31] Inzarilli, argues for two kinds of representatives: 1) those who advise on technical and operational matters, and 2) those who evaluate the benefits of membership. When this distinction is not made, Inzarilli argues, the objectivity and judgments of representatives are open to question.

[32] Inadequate attention to management was apparent at the birth of several consortia. The typical case began with high spirits and hopes about benefits and a belief that consortia management was a simple job with qualifications limited to some administrative experience and technical competence in R&D.

Consensus Conclusions Are Suspect: Most consortia rely on member committees for oversight and information about member needs and constraints. However, reliance on consensus generally:

    a. Satisfies as many members as possible by doing a little of everything

    b. Ends up with logic and data that is so abstract as to not be of use, and

    c. Favors noncontroversial goals unlikely to generate innovation.

In some cases, members are from different industry segments and this promotes unwieldy structures that paralyze strategy. For example, one consortium had at least three layers of committees: 1) a Technical Board of department heads for decisions on technical subjects, 2) a Program Board of vice-presidents for decisions on broad subject areas, and 3) a Policy Board up of company presidents for decisions on overall strategy. The perspectives of each committee had value. However, each level insisted on veto power over allocations and this limited planning to consensus judgment that led to an inflexible and abstract program infamous for ineffective and conservative studies.

Reliance on independent consortium managers is the necessary alternative to decision making by consensus. Such reliance should not be universal but focused on signature programs of the consortium's top management that have been presented, but not necessarily approved by members.

Growth Must Not Sacrifice Identity: Consortia are prone to equate success with membership growth.   However, increased membership generally means increased diversity of interests and greater difficulty of program definition.   One consortium president recognized this issue and consciously limited new firms because he saw that the consortium performed more abstract studies as membership increased.

Other consortia were alert to *Identity Conservation* and not only restricted membership to one industry segment but rejected membership for supplier and customer companies.   For example, one consortium focused on textile mills and excluded fiber, machinery, and apparel companies. In addition to program sharpening, these exclusions minimized conflicts of interests. Other consortia dealt with the issue by admitting suppliers and customers to associate membership; that is, only to advisory membership.

Evidence Must Precede Cooperation: Planning is a prerequisite for cooperative projects (Grice, 1975). Projections are needed that define: 1) contributions of members, 2) abilities on project teams and advisory bodies, 3) benefits and costs of member support, and 4) criteria for trade-offs on conflicting objectives.   Milton Hochmuth's study of international R&D cooperation emphasizes the importance of data projections based on prior planning. He found that crisis or failure resulted when a consortium sought to extend the state-of-the-art without prior data on barriers and conflicts. Even in successful cases, Hochmuth found: "Learning to work together and resolve structural conflict ... took years to achieve and involved several serious crises (p. 189)."

Committees are productive when work is based on prior evidence of feasibility that provides guidance on alternative directions and trade-offs. Further planning is also necessary as projects achieve initial results. It is essential that such planning be carried out under the independent control of consortium management.[33]

One U.S. consortium, now defunct, is a clear example of the consequences of inadequate prior knowledge. Instead of work being based on technological planning, industry panels were used that received no preparation on possible programs. An outside observer of these panels noted that their "useless meetings foundered on repeated attempts to clarify and resolve conflicting objectives." Although several projects were eventually defined, the industry became disenchanted and withdrew its support.

Principles of Consortia Strategy

Collective Benefits Must Not Threaten Viability: An important principle of consortium management is that: Collective Benefits Need By-product Private Benefits: Projects must produce value for members and not just results available to a whole industry. Examples of private benefits that could follow from collective ones include: (1) exclusive reports for members before publication (2) private seminars before professional presentations, (3) restricted design manuals, (4) education for members only, (5) lobbying efforts with government, and (6) consulting on testing procedures and instrumentation.

The greater the share of collective benefits from consortium work, the greater the incentive of firms to take a 'free ride' and the greater the odds of consortium failure. A few viable consortia were found whose primary focus was on collective benefits. However, in every such case, threat or social coercion was present. Threats to the industry came from natural, competitive, or government sources. In cases of social pressure, the consortia were formed by a clique of leaders during a unique period such as one of high prestige for scientific work. Such consortia experienced rising member dissatisfaction as time went on and withdrawal once the threat or pressure lessened and private benefits did not emerge.

The U.S. Department of Commerce failed to understand this principle when it encouraged the Apparel Research Foundation (ARF) to organize by providing both seed money but with a proviso that results were to be available to the entire apparel industry. Within a few years of the expiration of government funding, industry support withdrew and the consortium was dissolved.

---

[33] Consortia managers must use independent funds to develop new possibilities rather than merely support the technical interests of their staffs. The British government has long given substantial grants to RAs (approximately 25% of most budgets) believing funds could be used to explore innovative projects. The grants came under strong attack, however, when it was clear they were used to fund research in well-established areas of academic interest to consortia staffs (Jones and Johnson

Mancur Olson's Theory of Collective Goods also suggests that membership dues be proportional to the benefits each obtains (dues based on: sales volume, production volume, number of employees, etc.). The theory discourages special appropriations, honorary memberships, and gifts on grounds that these are only successful if coupled with social coercion. Data on funding patterns (Table 45) support Olson's theory. Annual assessments for R&D are the most important source of funds and special assessments and gifts are minor sources.[34]

Table 45

Funding Patterns at Consortia*

Primary Fund	N	%	Annual Budget <$100K	<$500K	$1M +
Annual Assessment	33	37	17	9	8
Other Appropriation	27	30	6	3	2
Project Assessments	8	9	2	0	1
Annual Project Assessment	8	9	6	4	3
Gifts	5	6	2	0	1
Other	9	4	0	4	0

(N = 90)

* Data are from Question 20. Primary funding refers to the one source of at least 40%.

Growth refers to budgets that were both greater than $100,000 and increasing.

Interaction and Private Benefits: Placing competent representatives on advisory committees can be more expensive and more important to consortia success. Providing such representation may seem to contradict Olson's theory since results of committee work are collective benefits available to all. The contradiction is only apparent, however, because of such private benefits from involvement as:

a. Detailed knowledge of projects (results, experiments, know-how', etc.),

b. Faster knowledge of project results,

c. Influence over projects, services, and staff assignments,

d. Influence on the direction and publication of operational tests, and

e. Personal familiarity with consortia staff who may serve as consultants.

---

[34] The category "Appropriations from Other Funds" applies mostly to organizations with R&D as a minor activity. Members of such organizations pay annual dues apportioned to R&D and other activities.

Interest in private benefits is growing in other countries. For example, Jones and Johnson's study of English RAs notes the importance of "repayment work" (p.29) defined as a "request of an individual member for specific assistance".[35]   Such repayment work was 14.1% of RA budgets in 1963 and 23.7% in 1970.

The data of this study are not comparable because they only include funding for R&D and no other activities such as information services.   Nevertheless, repayment work is less important; Table 46 shows repayment work at 9.2% of the average budget.[36]

Table 46

Fund Sources at Consortia *

Source of Funds	Avg. % of Budget
a. R&D Annual Assessment	37.9
j. General Fund Appropriation	32.0
b. Specific Project Assessment	12.9
i. Special Gifts & Grants	5.3
c. Member Contracts and Project	3.6
k. Other Sources	3.1
d. U.S. Government Contracts & Grants	2.9
f. Non-Member Project Contracts	1.3
e. State & Local Gov. Grants & Contracts	0.5
g. Other Assoc. Grants & Contracts	0.5
h. Foreign Grants & Contracts	0.5

*Data are from Question 20

Threat Reduction Is Temporary: R&D that relaxes a regulation will be collective for all firms.   It is also difficult to restrict benefits on consumer and worker health and safety since support for such work is unlikely unless members share a sense of threat from regulatory action.   Both theory and history show that such work will only be maintained as long as the threat exists.

---

[35] Jones also notes growth in group projects but does not provide data on extent. Group project funding is similar to project assessments in Table 51 (12.9% of U.S. consortia budgets).

[36] This total is obtained from Table 51 by adding data from categories c, d, e, f, g, and part of k (.4% was related to "fees).

An example of threat induced regulatory work occurred in the textile industry. A lung disease, Byssinosis, was thought to stem from cotton dust found in textile mills. When the federal government considered tougher dust standards, the industry's largest company began an R&D program on dust even though it was clear that results would be made freely available. Given the collective nature of the benefits from R&D on Byssinosis, the program was transferred to a trade association but was only supported while the threat existed. The program was terminated once the threat was reduced.

Technical work on environmental and health/safety issues may gain member support if consortia managers assure By-product benefits such as:

a. Advance warning and expert interpretation on legislation,

b. Consultation on cost/effectiveness of equipment and procedures for minimizing environmental and health/safety problems,

c. Evaluations of new technologies for compliance, and

d. Assistance on compliance issues for plant operations.

The message for government is that firms only support cooperative R&D to the extent that they receive private benefits. Government may feel that cooperation has promise in environmental and health areas. However, if government supports collective action, it must also support private by-products. The most obvious government support is research grants which must include funds for services to members. Government may also decrease requirements for shared funding in contracts. This recommendation may appear counter to a principle that government funding should not be free. However, industry is funding a competent consortia Lab that will have value for societal needs.

Summary: Consortia managers must steer a course between the Scylla of competitive value and the Charybdis of collective benefits. Members prefer that projects with targeted competitive benefits be pursued by the firms gaining the benefits. Members prefer to not support projects with collective benefits that could give some a 'free ride'. The often-difficult to discern middle ground is a project with sufficient by-product benefits.

Some consortia navigate the challenge with an overly safe and non-productive course such as only working on improvements to existing technology. An alternative course may be more difficult to manage but is also more likely to yield enduring support.

a. Offer a full range of private services to members (e.g., technical consultation, information services, improvement studies, technology evaluation, education, technical planning, etc.)

b. Enhance the by-product value of collective work with restricted work on exploratory research, governmental studies, systems research, and technical assistance to marketing.

Government Impediments to Consortia Laboratories

This section discusses government impediments to the contributions of consortia laboratories; that is, policies on grants and contracts, antitrust, and disclosure policy.

The Grants and Contracts Process: Unfortunately, consortia perceive the grants and contracts system to be an impediment to their success. Table 47 presents data on agencies that have given contracts or grants to consortia. The table shows that a significant number of labs received no grants or only participated in shared funding. Almost half the laboratories (13 of 27) have not received grants or contracts from government and only 6 of 27 laboratories have dealt with more than one agency. In fact, grants and contracts accounted for only three percent of consortia budgets.

Interviewees related several tales of woe about the government grants. In one case, a board of directors established a formal policy prohibiting acceptance of government grants. The ban was not tied to specific experiences. Instead, it was grounded in general arguments about "not being worth the trouble involved". The President of the consortium commented on the policy as follows:

> "I've been down that road and it's not worth the nonproductive effort in reporting and record keeping. We would need one or two additional people in our office to handle this. We would also end up obligating ourselves to all kinds of things like affirmative action plans, etc. We think like industry. A blanket, no-government-funds policy is the way to go. Rather than let the camel in the tent, we will go it alone and feel capable of doing so."

In another case, the laboratory's president noted that 50% of staff time was spent on grants even though they were 15% of the budget. When the Board heard of the situation, it urged ending grants. The President did not, however, because he felt grants gave the laboratory a voice in government policy.[37] Most industrial dissatisfaction was general in nature. Most comments alluded to: a) excessive paperwork, and b) perception that the review process for grants unfairly favored universities.[38] Only one laboratory raised a specific issue: differing agency policies on patents.

Government may use its purchasing power to pull laboratories into leadership positions only if those laboratories find such funding is attractive. Unfortunately, consortia laboratories find government discouraging.

---

[37] See the Industrial Research Laboratory report on <u>Institutional and Legal Constraints to Cooperative Energy Research and Development</u>.

[38] This last comment was often made in reference to the National Science Foundation. It was felt that NSF review panels were unfairly weighted with university researchers who did not understand consortia laboratories and their expertise in industrial practice.

Table 47

Government Contracts & Grants to Laboratories

Funding to Lab	# Labs	% Labs
Received no Funding	7	26
Lab shared funding only	6	22
Lab Funds from:		
One Agency	8	30
Two Agencies	1	4
Three Agencies	3	11
Four+ Agencies	2	7
	27	100%

Funding Agency	# Consortia	%
Environ. Protection Agency	6	43
Department of Agriculture	4	29
Department of Transportation	2	14
Housing and Urban Development	2	14
National Science Foundation	2	14
Department of Defense		
Navy	2	14
Air Force	1	7
Army	1	7
Veterans Administration	1	7
Health, Education & Welfare	1	7
Public Health Service	1	7
Office of Coal Research	1	7
National Bureau of Standards	1	7
Federal Aviation Authority	1	7
NASA	1	7

Consortia and Antitrust Policy: Consortia and members believe antitrust policy is not an impediment to their programs.   Consortia are aware of antitrust policy and they consider themselves within the law and its intent.   An absence of antitrust actions on consortia confirms that judgment.   While antitrust policy does not concern consortia, the perception was different at organizations with inactive programs.   The following discussion with one trade association typifies such beliefs.

> *Question*: Research on other countries suggests that cooperation is a valuable way of doing R&D. Why doesn't your industry support a cooperative program?

> *Response*: There are legal constraints to cooperation; namely antitrust policy.

> *Question*: Does that mean your organization has defined projects of value that counsel has advised you would violate antitrust legislation.

> *Response*: No. (No further explanation given.)

> *Question*: Are there specific cases that counsel has referred to about planning or conducting cooperative R&D in your industry?

> *Response*: No.

> *Question*: What reasoning supports concern that cooperative R&D might violate antitrust legislation?

> *Response*: General caution per Justice Department attention to our industry.

It is possible that antitrust is used as a rationalization for consortia failure to organize cooperative R&D.   The rationalization could obscure an industry's inability to define worthwhile R&D or that needs for R&D have not overcome concerns about government.   The key is that for cooperation to occur there must first be motivation. That means there must be perceived R&D results of value to the industry.   Relaxation of antitrust action cannot stimulate R&D where there is no R&D to stimulate.

Some publications of the Department of Justice ask if antitrust is an impediment to R&D (D. I. Baker).   These publications were responding to industrial arguments that public goods such as research on energy conservation should motivate relaxation of antitrust policies.   The relaxation sought would permit R&D between large firms.   The request may be legitimate but can only be answered by relating specific antitrust policies to specific R&D proposals.

It is possible that consortia are threatened by Justice Department clarifications of cooperative policy.   The Department's proposed conditions on cooperative efforts are one such example (see Table 48).   It is not clear if the Department insists that all these conditions be met.   But even if most of the conditions are mandatory, the effect on consortia could be disastrous.   It is possible the Department's policy deals with partnerships and not consortia.   The point is that partnerships are only one form of cooperation and government should have different policies for different forms.

Disclosure Policy: Federal policy insists that work funded by government be placed in the public domain. Unfortunately, this position forces benefits to be collective and attacks consortia viability. Disclosure may also pose an additional problem in requiring industry to make "background" work public; thus turning corporate secrets into a public good.

When government is a sole supporter and public good is the sole benefit, full disclosure is reasonable. It is entirely different when government provides funds that complement an industry's. In this situation, government and a consortium must negotiate partial disclosure. What must be avoided is full disclosure requirements that turn work into collective goods as when government disclosure policy killed did the Apparel Research Foundation.

Table 48
Antitrust Guidelines *

	Guidelines	Analysis
1	Consortia should operate independently on specific, competitive projects.	Most industries provided minimal support to single consortia.
2	Consortia should have parallel projects competing in one consortium.	Consortia budgets may be too small.
3	R&D should focus on basic research.	Basic research is likely a collective good.
4	Balance small and large firms in the consortium.	Small firms lack resources to use R&D. especially basic research.
5	Proprietary rights to resulting technology should be generally available.	Converts participatory benefits into collective goods.

*Source: U.S. Commerce Technical Advisory Board, Industry Collaboration in Energy R&D, 1974.

Government Inducements

Many consortia may not be capable of taking the steps needed for their full potential. However, this study concludes that it is in the society's interest to assist consortia to do so by providing inducements and support. This support is especially important in motivating, guiding, and assessing consortia on services that enhance R&D productivity including technology planning, technology exploration, and technology utilization.

Government Grants: Industrial funding will always be too meager for consortia seeking leadership to restructure industrial technologies. Government may legitimately respond here since society in general will benefit from restructuring that consortia lead.   While the value of funding leadership positions may be clear, the mechanism is not. Consortia laboratories simply do not attract the most competent and dynamic leaders. The laboratories encountered in this study are staffed by competent people, but most do little strategic thinking.   Programs that would encourage laboratories to do strategic planning, exploratory R&D, or even knowledge utilization face member resistance.   Finally, consortia laboratories are generally too small for strategic contributions. Even the larger consortia staffed by 30+ professionals have not been able to support strategic thinking.

A proactive role for government is pulling improved management and services into being via targeted grants. The work other students of R&D policy and this study have in mind is illustrated by the example of blow-molded apparel. The existing system in the textile/apparel industries (spin fiber into yarn, weave yarn to flat cloth, cut cloth into forms and sew forms into garments) has been in use for thousands of years (Heitmiller).   It is unrealistic to expect an industry with billions invested in an established system to render it obsolete unless the promise of return is strong.[39]

Government grants could require technology planning on system's change. Government should neither plan for nor develop new systems but it may encourage from universities and consortia to perform system analyses. Proposals should include explicit plans for relating the exploratory research to industry's existing capability.

A System of Consortia Laboratories: The system envisioned here is not only for member-based laboratories. Neither is it appropriate in every industry. The system should be strengthened by competition among laboratories of all types including laboratories at both universities and independent research organizations.[40]

The system envisioned here could also stimulate *Generic Technology* laboratories that cut across several industries. Such organizations already function on a limited scale including the: Welding Research Council, Flight Safety Council, and the Metal Properties Research Council. Jones notes that such systems-oriented laboratories are becoming more important among RAs in England. Perhaps they should also be more important in the U.S. as a mechanism for cooperative R&D in technologically intensive industries.   For example, chemical firms that might not cooperate in a Chemical Industry Consortium might value membership in a Process Control Institute.

Characteristics of a Consortium Laboratory focused on Generic Technology or one on an Exploratory Research on Alternative Systems should include:

---

[39] Important recent innovations in the industry all serve existing technologies: 1) shuttleless weaving, 2) open end spinning, 3) laser cloth cutting, and 4) the rink system of handling flat cloth.

[40] Examples of such organizations include Prodesco, Inc: and the Fabric Research Laboratory both of which serve the textile industry and KMS Industries, Inc. which performs work on fusion power.

a. Clear and stable identification with a specific field of technology;

b. Major activity in self-supporting technical services for its industry;

c. Deep ties to a specific, industrial constituency;

d. Professional management with competence in cooperative ventures;

e. Experience in the spectrum of activities of implementing technical ideas including planning, exploration, improvement, and utilization; and

f. Guarantees of independence in technology planning and exploration.

It is essential that government support be tendered for a total package of activities so that grants provide incentives for laboratories to improve their management and to broaden their involvement in strategic planning and alternative systems innovation. But the "total package" view of such grants should recognize that grants need to encourage a balanced mix of publicly supported collective benefits and private returns. Accordingly, there should be shared industry funding that assures a mix of private, participatory and collective benefits.

Laboratories that survive and grow in this competitive system will be ones that integrate activities across the full spectrum of: a) strategic thinking, b) forecasting, c) analysis, and d) innovation. The support packages will be an appropriate mix of: a) membership dues that cover participatory benefits, b) service fees that cover private benefits, and 3) government grants that cover collective benefits to the nation).[41]

Summary

This book ends with a proposal for a pluralistic and competitive system of consortia, university, and commercial laboratories funded by both government and industry. The industrial base for this system will provide experience with practice and commitments to specific fields essential for a cumulative growth of knowledge useful to society. Governmental support of the system will encourage strategic planning that defines attractive alternatives to existing technology, exploratory R&D on those technologies, and strategic programs to develop knowledge that motivates industrial development of the alternatives.

Consortia Laboratories have the potential to be leaders in the proposed system. The success of consortia laboratories in strategic work of national interest will depend on their ability to compete with other laboratories, correct managerial weaknesses, and formulate imaginative technological alternatives.

---

41 This study is not alone in emphasizing the importance of a full spectrum activity in cooperative organizations. The University of Wisconsin's Sociology Department, under Michael Aiken and Jerald Hage, stressed the failure of coordinating councils for mental health services to engage in the full spectrum of activities needed for success. Each source of support should also include funds, via overhead charges, for those activities that are useful By-products of benefits delivered.

BIBLIOGRAPHY

Ackerman, B. A. et al, *The Uncertain Search for Environmental Quality*, The Free Press, 1974.

Aiken, M. and Hage, J., "Organizational Interdependence and Intraorganizational Structure," .*American Sociological Review*, V. 63(1968), pp. 912-930.

_____, et al, *The Coordination of Services for the Mentally Retarded*, Report to the U.S. Department of Health, Education and Welfare, 1972.

Armstrong, J. S., and Overton, T., "Methods of Estimating Non Response Bias in Mail Surveys," *Wharton School Working Paper*, February 26, 1971.

Arnold, P.M., "Why Not Try Cooperative Research," *Harvard Business Review*, July - August, 1954, pp. 115-122.

Baker, D. I., "Remarks to the Conference Board's 13th Annual Antitrust Conference New York, March 7, 1974.

Balmforth, D. and Tewksbury, C. G.," EPAs Effluent Guidelines: A Cooperative Program," *Textile Chemist and Colorist*, July, 1974, pp. 35-38.

Battelle Institute, *Research by Cooperative Organizations*, National Science Foundation Report 56-12, 1956.

Blau, P.M. and Scott, W. R., *Formal Organizations*, Chandler Publishing, 1962.

Bodensteiner, W. D., *Information Channel Utilization Under Varying Research and Development Conditions*, Ph.D. Dissertation, University of Texas at Austin, 1970.

Bradley, J. F., *The Role of Trade Associations and Professional Business Societies in America*, Pennsylvania State University Press, 1965.

Bright, J. R., *Research, Development and Technological Innovation*, Richard Irwin, 1964 (see the "Photon" cases).

Business Week, "The Difficult Job of Shutting Off Noise," February 2, 1976, pp. 17-18.

Churchman, C.W., *The Design of Inquiring Systems: Basic Concepts of Systems and Organizations*, Basic Books, Inc., New York, NY, 1971

Cooper, A. C. and Schendel, D., "Strategic Responses to Technological Threats," *Business Horizons*, February, 1976, pp. 61-69.

deStritu, J.V.Y., "Defense Organizations and Alliances," in *Interorganizational Decision Making*, edited by M. Tuite, R. Chisholm and M. Radnor, Aldine, 1972.

Deutsch, M., "A Theory of Cooperation and Competition," *Human Relations*, V.2 (1949), pp. 129-152.

Deutsch, M. '*The Resolution of Conflict*, Yale University Press, 1973.

Encyclopedia of Associations, 8th edition, edited by M. Fisk, Gale Research Company, 1973.

Enos, J. L., *Petroleum Progress and Profits*, MIT Press, 1962.

Festinger, L., *A Theory of Cognitive Dissonance*, Row-Peterson, 1957.

Frohlick, N., Oppenheimer, J.A., and Yourig, O. R., *Political Leadership and Collective Goods*, Princeton University Press, 1971.

Gordon, T.J. *The Electric Power Research Institute: A Potential Case Study in Institutional Innovation*, Denver Research, 1973.

Grice, Paul, His work in 1975 is summarized in the following reference; *Studies in the Way of Words,* Harvard University Press, 1989.

Haefele, E. T., *Representative Government and Environmental Management*, Johns Hopkins University Press, 1973.

Heitmiller, R. F., "The Force of Change," *Modern Textiles*, September 1972, pp., 19-24.

Hochmuth, M.S., *Organizing the Transnational*, Leiden, Holland: A. W. Sijthoff, 1974.

Hollomon, H. J., "Technology in the United States: Issues and Options for the 1970s," *Technology Review*, June-August, 1972.

Industrial Research Institute, *Institutional and Legal Constraints to Cooperative Energy Research and Development*, U.S. Commerce Technical Advisory Board, March, 1975 (PB-240-929).

Inzerilli, G., *Interorganizational Cooperation in the Research Field*, Wharton School, Management Department Working Paper, 1976.

Joglekar, P., "Developments in the Theory of Voluntary Provision of Collective Goods," Conference of the Society for General Systems Research, Denver, Colorado, February, 1977.

Johnson, P. S., *Cooperative Research in Industry*, Martin Robertson & Co. Ltd. (England), 1973.

Jones, R. H., *Research Associations: - The Changing Pattern*, Centre for the Study of Industrial Innovation (England), 1972.

Kelly, P., Kranzberg, M. et al, *Technological Innovation: A Critical Review of Current Knowledge*, Georgia Tech, 1975.

Lawrence, P. R., and Lorsch, J. W., *Organization and Environment*, Richard D. Irwin, 1969.

Litwak, E. and Hylton, L., "Interorganizational Analysis: A Hypothesis on Coordinating Agencies," *Administrative Science Quarterly*, March, 1962.

Marwell, G. and Schmitt, D. R., *Cooperation: An Experimental Analysis*, Academic Press, 1975.

Mansfield, E., et al, *Research and Innovation in the Modern Corporation*, W.W. Norton & Co., 1971.

Mott, B.J.F., *Anatomy of a Coordinating Council: Implications for Planning*, University of Pittsburgh Press, 1968.

Nelson, R. R., Peck, M. J., and Kalachek, E. D., *Technology, Economic Growth and Public Policy*, Brookings Institute, 1967.

Nisbet, R. A., "Cooperation," in *International Encyclopedia of the Social Sciences*, edited by D. Sills, Macmillan Free Press, 1968, pp. 384-390.

Olson, M., *The Logic of Collective Action*, Harvard University Press, 1965.

_____, and Zeckhauser, R., "An Economic Theory of Alliances," *Review of Economics and Statistics*, V. 68 (1966), pp. 266-279.

Ozol, M. A. et al, "Study to Determine the Feasibility of an Experiment to Transfer Technology to the Crushed Stone Industry," Report MML TR-74-26c, Martin Marietta Labs, 1974.

Schacter, S., *The Psychology of Affiliation*, Stanford University Press, 1959.

Schein, E. H., *Organizational Psychology*, Prentice Hall, 1965.

Schermerhorn, J. R., "Determinants of Interorganizational Cooperation," *Academy of Management Journal*, V. 18 (1975), pp. 846-856.

Science Trends, "NSF/Industry Research," October 11, 1976.

Shatz, J. E., "Affiliation and Informal Choice as a Function of Fear and Joy," Doctoral Dissertation, University of Pennsylvania, 1967.

Toch, H., *The Social Psychology of Social Movements*, Bobbs-Merrill, 1965.

Tuite, M., Gusholm, R. and Radnor, M., *Interorganizational Decision Making*, Aldine, 1972.

Turk, H., "Comparative Urban Structure from an Interorganizational Perspective," *Administrative Science Quarterly*, V. 18 (1972), pp. 37-55.

U.S. Government, Office of the President, *Economic Report of the President*, U.S. Government Printing Office, 1971, pp. 125-130.

U.S. Senate, "Technical Research Activities of Cooperative Associations", Study of the Subcommittee on Patents, Trademarks, and Copyrights of the Committee on the Judiciary, 85th Congress, 2nd session, 1959.

Utterback, J. M., "Innovation in Industry and the Diffusion of Technology," *Science*, V. 183 (1974), pp. 620-626.

Van de Ven, A. H., and Loenig, R., "Pairwise Inter-Agency Relationships: Theory and Preliminary Findings," *Wharton School, Management Department Working Paper*, February 15, 1976.

_____, "A Design for Studying Interorganizational Relations, *Wharton School, Management Department Working Paper*, August 15, 1975.

Wilson, J. *Introduction to Social Movements*, Basic Books, 1973.

Woodward, F. N., *Structure of Industrial Research Associations*, Paris: Organization for Economic Cooperation and Development, 1965.

Yurow, J. and Brenner, F. C., *The Civilian Industrial Technology Program: A History and Evaluation*, U.S. National Bureau of Standards Report 10-182, 1969.

Zaltman, G., et al., *Innovations and Organizations*, John Wiley, 1973.

About Frank Wolek

My interests and style were influenced by where I was born, raised, and initially educated. I was born in 1935 in Brooklyn, New York; educated in Brooklyn Technical High School, the Colorado School of Mines (Geology), and Harvard Business School (doctorate in the management of science and technology). I've spent most of my career as a Professor of Management at several universities mostly at the Wharton School of the University of Pennsylvania and Villanova University (now an Emeritus Professor of Management). My contributions to others include service as Deputy Assistant Secretary of Science and Technology at the U.S. Department of Commerce and some 75 publications. I am happily married to Gloria Peez Wolek and we are proud of our four children and four grandchildren. I divide my time equally between homes in Florida and Philadelphia.

Other Books by Frank Wolek

Administering Research and Development with Charles Orth and Joseph Bailey, Homewood, IL: Richard D. Irwin, Inc., 1964.

Technology and Information Transfer, with Richard Rosenbloom, Boston, MA: Harvard Business School Division of Research, 1970.

Innovation Policy: Western Provinces of Canada, with Jean Eric Aubert, Francis Bonnet, Michael Proctor, and Veikko Vuorikari, Paris, France: OECD, 1988.

Governmental Innovation and New Agriculture, Villanova: Villanova Center for Agricultural Commerce, 1989.

Operations Management, with Matthew Liberatore and Robert Nydick, Villanova, PA.: LNW Publishing, 1998.

Government & Innovation: The Case of Agriculture, Audubon, PA.: Palantine Books, 2015.

My other publications may be located on the ResearchGate database at: https://www.researchgate.net/profile/Francis_Wolek

Staying In Touch with Frank Wolek

Linkedin: https://www.linkedin.com/pub/frank-wolek/50/32b/304

Webpage: http://www39.homepage.villanova.edu/francis.wolek/

APPENDIX A

QUESTIONNAIRE ON THE ROLE OF CONSORTIA IN THE NATIONAL R&D EFFORT

This survey is conducted by the University City Science Center (a consortium of 29 universities, colleges and schools in the Delaware Valley) under a grant from the National Science Foundation.

•   •   •

DEFINITIONS

These definitions are given in the order of appearance of the terms to which they apply. Please note that each definition also appears at the bottom of the page on which the term first appears.

Organization: The administrative entity and group of persons designated in the address to which this questionnaire was sent.

If your organization is a formal subunit of a larger entity, then question 2 should be answered for that larger entity and all other questions should be answered for the sub-unit given in the address.

If your organization has changed its name during the period covered by a specific question (e.g., during the past five years), that should have no effect on your answers.

If your organization has merged with or spun-off other organizations, please answer these questions with reference to the parent organization or the single, most identifiable unit in terms of its involvement in technical research and development.

Technical Research and Development (also called R & D): Includes the following: a) basic and applied research in the fields of science and engineering (e.g., chemistry, medicine, electrical engineering); b) design, development, and testing of prototype technologies; and c) improvement, testing, and analysis of products and processes to enhance technical performance, reduce cost, or improve safety and environmental impacts. This term does not include work aimed primarily at standardization, routine quality assurance, sales service, economic and marketing research or research in social and political science.

R & D Expenditures: The total dollars spent on both the direct and indirect costs (including depreciation) of doing technical research and development. This figure should include all expenditures on contracts and grants as well as for cooperative projects for your members.

Do not include funds of other organizations contributed to joint projects between your organization and theirs. Also do not include charges either for "General and Administrative" (i.e., non-R & D) overhead or capital budget commitments.

Please refer to actual accounting data in answering this question if that is possible.

Basic Research: Original investigations for the advancement of scientific knowledge which do not have specific commercial objectives, although they may be in fields of present or potential interest to a given industry. (Note this is the standard NSF definition used in all surveys by them of national R & D funding patterns).

Own Laboratories: Any laboratory installation including library, over which your organization exercises primary financial and supervisory control. The establishing of the laboratory facilities as a separate corporate identity does not necessarily remove that installation from such control by your organization.

Consortia: A formal association of three or more organizations (e.g., industrial firms) which cooperate in the funding and/or planning of technical research and development.

1. a) Name of organization_____

   b) Address_____

   c) Telephone number_____

   d) Name and title of the primary respondent to this questionnaire

   _____

2. Listed below are activities in which your **organization** may be involved. Please give your estimate of the relative importance of each activity in terms of your organization's contributions to its members over the past five years. Please check only the <u>one</u> most appropriate box for each activity.

   a) compilation of comparative statistics (e.g., salaries, safety, costs, etc.)

   not applicable ☐   *tertiary* ☐   *secondary* ☐   *primary* ☐

   b) assistance on accounting procedures and issues

   not applicable ☐   *tertiary* ☐   *secondary* ☐   *primary* ☐

   c) training and education of employees of member organizations or individual members

   not applicable ☐   *tertiary* ☐   *secondary* ☐   *primary* ☐

   d) assistance on employer-employee relations

   not applicable ☐   *tertiary* ☐   *secondary* ☐   *primary* ☐

   e) education of the general public and public relations activity

   not applicable ☐   *tertiary* ☐   *secondary* ☐   *primary* ☐

   f) relations with government

   not applicable ☐   *tertiary* ☐   *secondary* ☐   *primary* ☐

   g) marketing research

   not applicable ☐   *tertiary* ☐   *secondary* ☐   *primary* ☐

   h) **technical research and development**

   not applicable ☐   *tertiary* ☐   *secondary* ☐   *primary* ☐

   i) standardization of products and materials

   not applicable ☐   *tertiary* ☐   *secondary* ☐   *primary* ☐

   j) trade and/or professional publications

   not applicable ☐   *tertiary* ☐   *secondary* ☐   *primary* ☐

   k) organization of conventions, conferences or trade shows

   not applicable ☐   *tertiary* ☐   *secondary* ☐   *primary* ☐

   l) other (please describe) _____

   _____

   not applicable ☐   *tertiary* ☐   *secondary* ☐   *primary* ☐

Definitions

Organization: The administrative entity and group of persons designated in the address to which this questionnaire was sent.

If your organization is a <u>formal</u> <u>subunit</u> of a larger entity, then question 2 should be answered for that larger entity and all other questions should be answered for the sub-unit given in the address.

If your organization has <u>changed</u> <u>its</u> <u>name</u> during the period covered by a specific question (e.g., during the past five years), that should have no effect on your answers.

If your organization has <u>merged</u> <u>with</u> <u>or</u> <u>spun-off</u> other organizations, please answer these questions with reference to the parent organization or the single, most identifiable unit in terms of its involvement in technical research and development.

Technical Research and Development (also called R & D): Includes the following: a) basic and applied research in the fields of science and engineering (e.g., chemistry, medicine, electrical engineering); b) design, development, and testing of prototype technologies; and c) improvement, testing, and analysis of products and processes to enhance technical performance, reduce cost, or improve safety and environmental impacts. This term does <u>not</u> include work aimed primarily at standardization, routine quality assurance, sales service, economic and marketing research or research in social and political science.

3. Is your organization a subsidiary or other organizational subunit of any of the following organizations. (Note: in naming these organizations, please spell out the complete name rather than using acronyms or abbreviations).

    a) trade association (please state the name) _____

    b) university or college (please state the name) _____

    _____

    c) professional society (please state the name) _____

    _____

    d) commercial firm (please state the name) _____

    _____

    e) government agency (please state name) _____

    _____

    f) international association in your field of endeavor (please state name) _____

    _____

    _____

    g) other (please specify) _____

4. Does your organization presently fund and/or plan a program of technical research and development?

                          Yes _____   No _____

If your answer to question 4 is <u>Yes</u>, please skip question 5 and proceed to question 6.

If your answer to question 4 is <u>No</u>, please go on to question 5; then after answering question 5, return the questionnaire to us in the enclosed envelope.

5. Has your organization ever formally considered or actually conducted a program of technical research and development?

                          Yes _____   No _____

    Please note that the remaining questions should be answered <u>only</u> if your organization presently conducts a program of technical research and development.

6. Please estimate the number of years that your organization has been involved in a reasonably continuous program of technical research and development.   Number of Years _____

7. Please estimate the percentage of your organization's total budget for 1973 that was devoted to technical research and development.

                          _____%

8. Please estimate the total **R & D expenditures** of your organization for each of the years given below.

    a) Total for 1974 . . . .$ _____
    b) Total for 1973 . . . .$ _____
    c) Total for 1972 . . . .$ _____
    d) Total for 1971 . . . .$ _____
    e) Total for 1970 . . . .$ _____

Definitions

R & D Expenditures: The total dollars spent on both the direct and indirect costs (including depreciation) of doing technical research and development. This figure should include all expeditures on contracts and grants as well as for cooperative projects for your members.

Do <u>not</u> include funds of other organizations contributed to joint projects between your organization and theirs. Also do <u>not</u> include charges either for "General and Administrative" (i.e., non-R & D) overhead or capital budget commitments.

Please refer to actual accounting data in answering this question if that is possible.

9. Please indicate the method you utilized to derive your R & D expenditures in answer to question 8. Check the one most appropriate box below.

a) actual accounting data .... ☐

b) consensus of estimates of knowledgeable persons .... ☐

c) educated estimate of one person .... ☐

d) other (please specify) _____ .... ☐

10. Please estimate the percentage of your R & D expenditures devoted to **basic research** in each of the years given below.

% Allocated to Basic Research

a) 1974 .... _____ %

b) 1972 .... _____ %

c) 1970 .... _____ %

11. Listed below are several functions which your organization's R & D program may serve for its members. For each function, please place a check (√) on that point on the scale which in your judgment best estimates the percentage of total R & D projects in the past five years which have directly addressed this function. (Please note that since it is possible that projects addressed multiple functions, it is also possible for your answers to add to a total greater than 100%.

a) formulating theories to explain basic phenomena and properties of materials, processes and products (i.e., fundamental research).

```
L____|____|____|____|____|____|____|____|____|____|
0%         20%        40%        60%        80%        100%
```

b) developing prototype hardware for new processes to be used in manufacturing and related operations.

```
L____|____|____|____|____|____|____|____|____|____|
0%         20%        40%        60%        80%        100%
```

c) improving existing process technology

```
L____|____|____|____|____|____|____|____|____|____|
0%         20%        40%        60%        80%        100%
```

d) developing prototype hardware for new, marketable products

```
L____|____|____|____|____|____|____|____|____|____|
0%         20%        40%        60%        80%        100%
```

e) improving existing product technology

```
L____|____|____|____|____|____|____|____|____|____|
0%         20%        40%        60%        80%        100%
```

f) developing prototypes for new technologies which will promote occupational health and safety

```
L____|____|____|____|____|____|____|____|____|____|
0%         20%        40%        60%        80%        100%
```

g) improving existing technology for occupational health and safety

```
L____|____|____|____|____|____|____|____|____|____|
0%         20%        40%        60%        80%        100%
```

Definitions

Basic Research: Original investigations for the advancement of scientific knowledge which do not have specific commercial objectives, although they may be in fields of present or potential interest to a given industry. (Note this is the standard NSF definition used in all surveys by them of national R & D funding patterns).

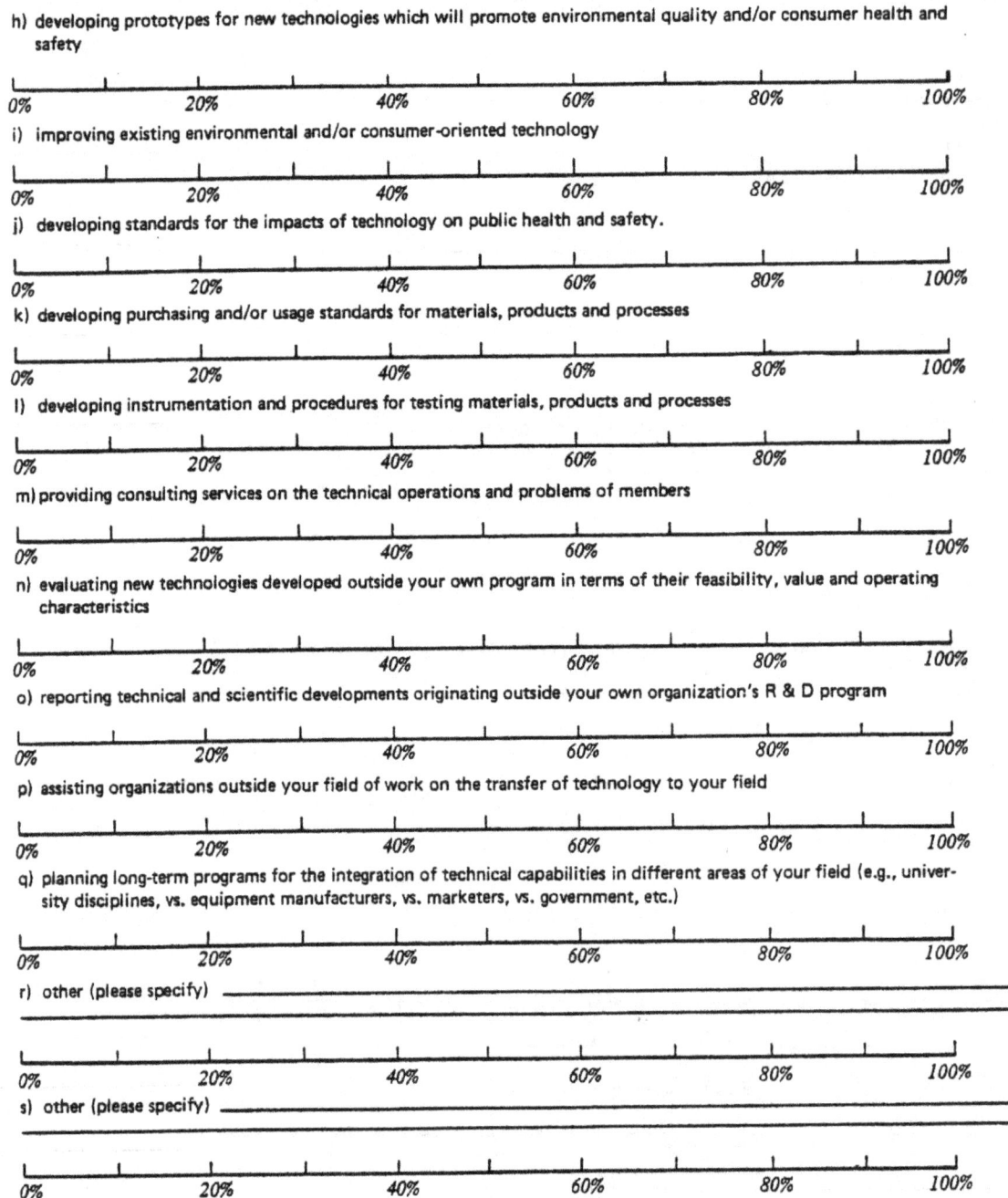

h) developing prototypes for new technologies which will promote environmental quality and/or consumer health and safety

```
L___|___|___|___|___|___|___|___|___|___|
0%      20%      40%      60%      80%     100%
```

i) improving existing environmental and/or consumer-oriented technology

```
L___|___|___|___|___|___|___|___|___|___|
0%      20%      40%      60%      80%     100%
```

j) developing standards for the impacts of technology on public health and safety.

```
L___|___|___|___|___|___|___|___|___|___|
0%      20%      40%      60%      80%     100%
```

k) developing purchasing and/or usage standards for materials, products and processes

```
L___|___|___|___|___|___|___|___|___|___|
0%      20%      40%      60%      80%     100%
```

l) developing instrumentation and procedures for testing materials, products and processes

```
L___|___|___|___|___|___|___|___|___|___|
0%      20%      40%      60%      80%     100%
```

m) providing consulting services on the technical operations and problems of members

```
L___|___|___|___|___|___|___|___|___|___|
0%      20%      40%      60%      80%     100%
```

n) evaluating new technologies developed outside your own program in terms of their feasibility, value and operating characteristics

```
L___|___|___|___|___|___|___|___|___|___|
0%      20%      40%      60%      80%     100%
```

o) reporting technical and scientific developments originating outside your own organization's R & D program

```
L___|___|___|___|___|___|___|___|___|___|
0%      20%      40%      60%      80%     100%
```

p) assisting organizations outside your field of work on the transfer of technology to your field

```
L___|___|___|___|___|___|___|___|___|___|
0%      20%      40%      60%      80%     100%
```

q) planning long-term programs for the integration of technical capabilities in different areas of your field (e.g., university disciplines, vs. equipment manufacturers, vs. marketers, vs. government, etc.)

```
L___|___|___|___|___|___|___|___|___|___|
0%      20%      40%      60%      80%     100%
```

r) other (please specify) _____

_____

```
L___|___|___|___|___|___|___|___|___|___|
0%      20%      40%      60%      80%     100%
```

s) other (please specify) _____

_____

```
L___|___|___|___|___|___|___|___|___|___|
0%      20%      40%      60%      80%     100%
```

12.a) Has your organization accepted grants and/or contracts for R & D from U.S. government agencies?

                                                Yes _____ No _____

  b) If your answer to 12a is yes, please name the agencies from which you have accepted grants and/or contracts

_____

_____

13.a) Has your organization given grants and/or contracts to agencies of the U. S. government for R & D to be performed by them?

                                                Yes _____ No _____

  b) If your answer to 13a is yes, please name the agencies to which you have given grants and/or contracts

_____

_____

14.a) Has your organization participated in jointly funded R & D with agencies of the U. S. government?

                                                Yes _____ No _____

  b) If your answer to 14a is yes, please name the agencies with which you have cooperated.

_____

_____

  c) If your answer to 14a is yes, please estimate the percentage of your 1974 R & D expenditures that will be committed to cooperative projects with the U.S. government.

                                                           _____%

15. Has your organization accepted contracts from individual member organizations for proprietary R & D?

                                                Yes _____ No _____

16. Has your organization accepted contracts from groups of members for proprietary R & D?

                                                Yes _____ No _____

17. Has your organization accepted contracts from non-member organizations (other than governmental) for proprietary R & D?

                                                Yes _____ No _____

18. Please estimate the percentage of your 1974 R & D expenditures that will be spent at each of the following places. (Note: the percentages requested here relate to the dollar sum given in answer to item 8a)

  a) Your **own laboratories** .... _____%

  b) member organization laboratories (excluding those of government agencies)............................. _____%

  c) college or university laboratories .... _____%

  d) unaffiliated not-for-profit research organizations such as Battelle Institute .... _____%

  e) commercial laboratories or research organizations such as A. D. Little, Inc. .... _____%

  f) U. S. government laboratories, ... _____%

  g) non-member, industrial laboratories .... _____%

  h) laboratories of another association, society or research institute .... _____%

  i) other, (please specificy) _____

_____ _____%

                                                              100%

Definitions

Own Laboratories: Any laboratory installation including library, over which your organization exercises primary financial and supervisory control. The establishing of the laboratory facilities as a separate corporate identity does not necessarily remove that installation from such control by your organization.

19. If your organization operates its own laboratory
   a) How many professional engineers and scientists are currently employed? _____ /

   b) Is that laboratory located immediately near a university campus?
                                                   Yes _____   No _____
   c) Is that laboratory located near a major industrial center for your field of work?
                                                   Yes _____   No _____

20. Please estimate the percentage of your organization's 1974 R & D expenditures which will be obtained from each of the following sources:
   a) annual or other regular assessments of your members given explicitly for R & D . . . .   _____ %
   b) assessments of your members for specific, non-proprietary R & D projects . . . .   _____ %
   c) contracts from members for specific, proprietary R & D projects . . . .   _____ %
   d) U.S. government grants or contracts . . . .   _____ %
   e) state and local government grants or contracts . . . .   _____ %
   f) contracts from non-member, U. S. companies for specific R & D projects . . . .   _____ %
   g) contracts and grants from other associations, societies and/or research institutes . . . .   _____ %
   h) contracts and grants from foreign or international organizations . . . .   _____ %
   i) special gifts and/or grants . . . .   _____ %
   j) appropriations from general purpose funds of your organization (note: appropriate only if R & D is one of several functions of your organization) . . . .   _____ %
   k) other sources (please specify) _____
   _____   _____ %

                                                                              100%

21. Please estimate the percentage of members directly contributing to your organization's R & D budget for 1974   _____ %
22. Please estimate the percentage of foreign organizations directly contributing to your organization's R & D budget for 1974   _____ %
23. Please indicate the extent to which your organization seeks out foreign organizations for membership by checking the one most appropriate box.

   a) we do not accept foreign members . . . . ☐

   b) we accept foreign members but the initiative rests with them . . . . ☐

   c) foreign memberships are largely a by-product of professional activities conducted in other countries . . . . ☐

   d) we make explicit but moderate efforts to recruit foreign members . . . . ☐

   e) we make explicit and active efforts to recruit foreign members . . . . ☐

   f) Other (Please specify) _____
   _____ . . . . . . ☐

24.a) Is your organization a member or otherwise affiliated with an international association for R & D in your field?
                                                   Yes _____   No _____

   b) If your answer to 24a is yes, please give the full name of that association on the following lines _____
   _____

94

25. Please estimate the percentage of ideas for R & D projects (submitted in the past year) originating from each of the following groups.

a) staff (i.e., salaried employees) of your organization. . . . . ____%
b) representatives of members who serve on committees of your organization . . . . ____%
c) employees of member organizations (other than representatives on committees) . . . . ____%
d) individual persons holding membership in your organization . . . . ____%
e) employees of non-member organizations working on R & D funded by your organization . . . . ____%
f) persons submitting unsolicited proposals (other than those working on projects funded by your organization) . . . ____%
g) other (please specify.) _____

_____ . . . . . ____%

‾‾‾‾‾‾‾
100%

26. Please list the names of one to three **consortia** engaged in technical research and development (exclusive of your own organization) which you believe make especially significant contributions to technical progress in their fields.

1. _____
2. _____
3. _____

27. If you would like to receive a copy of the report on our study, please check the following box. ☐

THANK YOU VERY MUCH FOR YOUR COOPERATION

Definitions

Consortia: A formal association of three or more organizations (e.g., industrial firms) which cooperate in the funding and/or planning of technical research and development.

95

www.ingramcontent.com/pod-product-compliance
Lightning Source LLC
Chambersburg PA
CBHW080826180526
45168CB00006B/2590